The Antiquities of Middlesex; Being a Collection of the Several Church Monuments in That County

THE
ANTIQUITIES
OF
MIDDLESEX;

Being a Collection of the several

Church Monuments

IN THAT

COUNTY:

ALSO

An Historical Account of each

CHURCH and *PARISH*;

WITH

The Seats, Villages, and Names of the most Eminent Inhabitants, &c.

PART I. Beginning with *Chelfea* and *Kenfington.*

Now in the Prefs, PART II. Will Contain the Parifhes of
Fulham, Hammerfmith, Chifwick, and *Afton.*

LONDON,

Printed by *W Redmayne* for *S. Keble* at the Great *Turk's-Head* in *Fleetftreet, D Browne*
at the *Black Swan* and *Bible* without *Temple bar, A Roper* at the *Black Boy* in *Fleetftreet,*
R Smith at the *Angel* and *Bible* without *Temple-bar,* and *F Coggan* in the *Inner-*
Temple-Lane, MDCCV.

TO

HANS SLOANE M. D.

FELLOW and SECRETARY

OF THE

ROYAL SOCIETY

This Collection of the *Funeral Monuments,
Inscriptions*, &c. in the COUNTY of
Middlesex, Part I. *viz.* of the Churches
and Parishes of *Chelsea* and *Kensington*

Is Humbly Dedicated

By

His most Humble Servant

J. Bowack.

TO

TO THE

READER.

WE *shall not attempt an* Encomium *upon* History *in general, nor upon any particular* Branches *of it, to which our* Undertaking *more nearly relates, since most of those* Learned Men, *who have* enrich'd *the World with the Accounts of past* Actions, *have at the same time, accurately evinc'd the* Usefulness *and* Excellency *of such kind of* Knowledge; *which is, and ever was, in the highest esteem among all* Persons, *and will continue so to* Posterity; *an insatiable Desire of knowing what is past, as well as what is to come, being so fix'd in* Humane Nature, *as never to be eradicated. Nor shall we bespeak the* Readers Favour *in behalf of the Subject since the* Funeral Monuments *and* Inscriptions *of* Grutterus, Schraderus, Swertius, *and our own Country-men* Weaver, Hoveden, &c. *have been so universally esteem'd; and the kind* Reception *they met with from the Common Wealth of* Learning, *is an* Evidence *of the Sense they have of the* Usefulness *of such* Performances. *But our present* Design *is fairly to advertise the* Reader *of the* Cause *and* Method *of our* Undertaking, *that he may know what he is to expect, and may be pre-acquainted with such things, as might else give him* Cause *to mistake our* Design.

Mr. Weaver's Funeral Monuments *of* Great Britain, *Publish'd about the Year* 1631, *was very well recev'd then, and has continued in such* Reputation *ever since, that there's hardly any that does not speak respectfully of that* Author. *But such has been the* Alteration *in our* Language *since his time, (however this* Subject *may be approv'd of, as being a curious* Miscellany *of the most pleasant Part of* History, *viz. the* Lives *and* Deaths *of such* Illustrious Persons, *as have appear'd in our* Island *for so many Ages past, nay the very* Foundation *of it, there being nothing inscrib'd on the* Monuments *of the Defunct, relating to their Births, Deaths, or Actions, but what is undoubtedly true;) yet his Style and manner of Writing appears now obsolete, and is not so well relish'd by the Nice Palates of this* Age, *as the more modern Performances:* Besides *(not to detract from the deserv'd* Character *of that Industrious* Author*) as in some* Places *he wanders strangely from his* Design, *and frequently makes long* Excursions *into* Insipid Monkish Stories, *which have not such certainty in 'em as could be wish'd, and does not come within the reach of his* Title, *so in other places, he does not seem to be particular enough, some* Churches *of good* Antiquity, *not being taken notice of at all, and others crowded with In-scriptions he often very slightly touches, and of Twenty* Monuments *it may be, only observes one or two, and in them oftentimes (taking the best part of his* Matter *upon* Trust*) the* Inscriptions *are not so justly transcrib'd as they ought*

A   *to* to be. His Readers are likewise much surpris'd, when expecting the Monuments of Great Britain, they only find a Discourse of Funerals in general, and of the Monuments of the Dioceses of Canterbury, Rochester, London and Norwich: for what Causes the rest were omitted, we are altogether ignorant of, he himself giving no Account of them.

The Inscriptions which happen to be in Latin or French, &c. he has not Translated, by which means the English Reader is depriv'd of that satisfaction he might reasonably have expected from such a Collection: So that several good Judges upon a careful perusal of what he has written on this Subject, (though they allow him to have taken a great deal of Pains in clearing the Rubbish, and gone a great way in this untrodden Path with good success, yet do justly imagine he has left room for others to come after him, and make great and useful Improvements upon his first Endeavours.

But admitting he had compleated this Subject to his time, and in all respects been so correct that no Errors had crept in, nor Omissions happen'd, yet so many Worthy Men have made their Exit since that time, that tracing over only those very Places he has taken notice of, would make a Supplement exceeding in bulk his Volume: How many Magnificent Monuments have been Erected within the Circle of few Years? and how many have expir'd in the Bed of Honour, since the Year 1630, in defence of their Prince, Religion, or Country, against profess'd Enemies abroad, or more dangerous ones at home; whose Memories ought eternally to live and flourish? we hope therefore the Premises consider'd, the publick will have so favourable an Opinion of our Undertaking, as to think we have not unnecessarily engag'd in it.

It were to be wish'd indeed, that this Argument had been undertaken by some of the most celebrated Modern Pens; and 'tis somewhat surprising, that in this Fertile Age when all other Subjects are almost worn threadbare, this alone should lie neglected! 'Twas this consideration that inclin'd us to make some Attempts this way, which (notwithstanding all we can say,) will no doubt admit of large Essays from other hands.

We don't intend to wander in so large a Field as Mr. Weaver did; for fear we should be justly chargeable with his Faults; but shall confine our selves only at present to the narrow Compass of the County of Middlesex, every individual Parish though never so small in the Course of our Proceedings we shall trace, and with the greatest care Examine and Collect our Materials.

The City of London and all its Churches and Monuments, being generally known we don't think proper to begin with first; but shall set out from the first Parish beyond the Verge of the Bills of Mortality towards the West, which is Chelsea; and after we have taken those by the River Thames to the Western limits of the County, we design to Visit the Northern Parts of it, till we meet that River again in the East; and in the Course of this our Perambulation the Reader may expect all the Epitaphs and Funeral Inscriptions of Persons Interr'd in this County, who have made any Figure in the World, that either for Language, Antiquity, or Humour are remarkable shall be carefully transcribed on the spot, and that such as are in Latin, &c. shall be done into English, with a short Account of the Lives of the Deceased, if of any Note.

A

A Description of such Monuments as are Curious, and an Estimate of their Value; also all things that are worthy of Observation within each Church.

Some Account of the Antiquity and Structure of every Church, the Alterations that has happen'd since its Founding, the most considerable Benefactions, the Name of its Patron, and Value of the Living.

A Description of all such things within each Parish as are Worthy of Remark, whether Ancient or Modern; all their Fine Seats, Mannors, and eminent Inhabitants; also an Account of the Growth or Decrease of their Towns or Villages.

We have been careful in Treating of these Subjects, to consult the most approved Authors that have Written on 'em; and have been much assisted by the Manuscripts and Papers communicated to us by several Worthy Gentlemen; but our Undertaking being so large, and requiring our observations of some things not yet taken notice off, we were oblig'd to consult the most Intelligent Persons in each Parish, whose Kindness we have publickly acknowledg'd with their several Informations.

Whatever defects or want of Embellishment appears in our Style, we hope will in some measure be made up, in the variety and certainty of our Relations; and if after all our Care in searching for Truth, any Errors have happen'd to creep in, we hope the Judicious will make allowances for 'em, considering the Difficulties and Latitude of our Undertaking; however, upon better Information we shall be very ready to Correct 'em, and publickly acknowledge such a Kindness.

Amongst the several Reasons that induc'd us to Publish this Work in Parts, this was not the least considerable, that we believ'd 'twou'd be more to the satisfaction of the Publick, since some Gentlemen as may be dispos'd to have an Account of their own Parish, or of such as contain the Monuments of their Ancestors, &c. may not be inclin'd to have that of the whole County, and for such as desire to have all Complete, the whole are to be bound up at the Years end together in a Volume.

We shall not trouble the Reader with any thing further, only desire his candid perusal of this our first Attempt, and assure him, if due Encouragement be given, he may not only expect the whole County of Middlesex to be Publish'd in the Method we have propos'd, but likewise many other Counties that have not been attempted by any other Hands.

ER-

ERRATA

BEsides several literal Faults and Miftakes in pointing, which by the hurry of the Prefs have crept into thefe Sheets, there has happen'd the following Omiffions and Errata's, which the Reader is defir'd to obferve and correct before he proceeds, and great care will be taken in our other Publications to give him as little trouble this way as poffible.

Page 3 *l* 43 *r* She will rife again by God's Permiffion, p 4 *l* 21 add King's Chaplain, p 8 *l* 32 after deceas'd *r* and for his own ufe (when he fhall dye) *Cb Chyne* Efq, Lord of this Mannor of *Chelfea* (which was purchas'd by the large Fortune of his Wife) took care that this fubterraneous Repofitory of Afhes fhould be built This was dedicated the third day of the Calends of *Nov* 1669 I befeech thee Almighty God that fhe may quietly reft here Buried till the Refurrection of all I flefh, *Amen* p 13 *l* 31 from the bottom *r.* three.times, *ib. l* 21 *r* Converfation, *ib* laft line *r* Dr *Langford*, p 14 *l* 5 *r* Figures, *ib l* 27 omit Officers Names, p 15 *l* 5 *r.* Dr. *Morley*, *ib l* 14 *r* Mr *Jofias Prieft*, *ib l* 27 *r.* Commiffaries for Commiffioners, p 19 *l* 12 *r. praeclarum*, *ib l* 27 *r Pompa*, *ib.* 36 but Death regards not thefe things, p 23 laft line *r.* any of the

---

ADVERTISEMENT.

THis Undertaking having receiv'd great Improvements from the Manufcripts and Informations of feveral Learned Gentlemen fince it was firft began, the World may expect more variety than was promis'd in the Title Page : And the Undertakers hereby affure all fuch Gentlemen as have made Collections on this Subject (efpecially of fuch Monuments whofe Infcriptions are defac'd or loft) that if they will pleafe to tranfmit their Obfervations in time to any of 'em, with their Names, they fhall be thankfully inferted.

All fuch Gentlemen as are difpos'd to encourage this Undertaking, by giving Cuts of their Seats or Monuments, &c. are defir'd to give timely Notice to the Undertakers and they fhall be neatly done at reafonable Rates, and Bound up with this Work in a Volume when the whole County is completed.

THE

THE
ANTIQUITIES
OF
MIDDLESEX, &c.

CHELSEA.

THE firſt Place that offers itſelf beyond the Verge of the Bills of Mortality towards the Weſt, is *Chelſea* ; a Town ſweetly ſituated upon a riſing gravelly Ground, on the Northern Banks of the Thames , adorn'd with a handſome Church, and ſeveral ſtately Piles of Building, (particularly that Magnificent Hoſpital, founded by King *Charles* II beautify'd with ſeveral large and pleaſant Gardens,) and celebrated for the Reſidence of many of the Nobility and Gentry , but of theſe more at large in their proper Place, our Method obliging us firſt to conſider

THE CHURCH.

This Church dedicated to St. *Luke*, appears to have been very Ancient, by the old Wall now ſtanding on the North ſide, built of Flint and rough Stone, confuſedly heap'd together, as well as by the Teſtimony of the moſt Antient Inhabitants, who remember it before the Rebuilding.

In the Year 1667, the Old Church which was much decay'd, being too ſmall to contain the Congregation, (grown very large by the vaſt Increaſe of Buildings, about that time in the Town,) it was agreed by the Pariſhioners that part of it ſhould be demoliſhed, and that ſuch Additions and Alterations ſhould be made as was neceſſary, for their decent Accommodation ; accordingly the ſhatter'd Tower, and Weſt End of the Church was pull'd down, and the North and South Sides, carried ſeveral Yards towards the Weſt, by Two Back Walls At the Weſt End was Built a lofty Square Tower of Brick, being in all about 80 Feet from the Ground.

The Walls of the whole Church were Rais'd, the Windows Inlarg'd, the old Parts Beautified, the inſide new Pav'd and Pew'd, the Church-yard conſiderably Rais'd and Incloſ'd, with a high Wall of Brick , and moſt of this done at the voluntary Charge of the Inhabitants, and the whole Roof, Lead, Timber, &c thereunto belonging, at the ſole Coſt of the Lady *Jane Cheyne*

The Church was alſo furniſh'd with all the neceſſary Ornaments, and the Steeple with a good Ring of Six Bells, by the great Bounty of ſeveral of the Noble and Worthy Inhabitants.

Having thus given a brief Account of the Church, we proceed to take a Survey of its Monuments within, which notwithſtanding the ſo conſying is before, have been carefully preſerv'd and kept entire

The firſt we begin with is the Monument of Sir *Thomas Moore*, (a Man of univerſal Learning) which is the only one, Mr. *Weaver* in his *Funeral Monument* takes notice of in this Church, though at that time there were ſeveral ſtanding more Noble than this, the Memory of which ought to have been carefully tranſmitted to Poſterity

In the CHANCEL

On the South ſide is a plain Monument of Black Marble, about Five Foot long, having on each ſide a ſmall Pillar , and on the Stone the following Inſcription

THomas Morus Vrbi Londinenſi, Familia non celebri, ſed honeſta natus, in Litteris utcunque verſatus, quum & Cauſas aliquot annos Juvenis egiſſet, in foro & in Vrbe ſui prædiun ſe que Exerçet ab invictiſſimo Rege Henrico Octavo (cui uni Regum omnium gloria prædicandaceſiget, ut fit Defenſor, qualem & gladio & calamo verè præſtitit, meritò vocitatus) delectus in aulam , delectuſque in conſilium Ei creatus Eques Proquæſtor primum, poſt Cancellarius Lancaſtria , tandem Angliæ, mire Prætn tipfis favore fačtus eft. Sed interim in publico Regis Senatu electus Orator Populi, praeterea legatus Regis nonnunquam fuit, alias alibi, poftremo vero Cameraci Comes & Collega junctus, Princeps legationis, Cutberto Tunftallo tui Londinenfi, mox Duneimenfi Epifcopo, quo viro vix habet orbis hodie quicquam erud'tius, prudentrue, melius Ibi inter fummos Orbis Chriftiani Monarchas rurfus referta fœdera, redditamq; mundo diu defideretam pacem laetiffimus vivit & legatus interfuit

Quam fuper pacem firment faxintque perennem

In hoc officiorum & honorum curfu, quum ita verfaretur, ut neque Princeps optimus operam ejus improbaret neque nobilibus effet invifus, nec incundus populo, Furibus autem & Homicidis moleftus Pater ejus tandem Job mules Morus Eques & in eum Judicum Ordinem, à Principe Occupatus, qui Regius concessus vocitur, homo civilis, suavis, innocens, mitis, mifericors, aequus, & integer, annis quidem gravis, fed corpore plusquam pro aetate vivido, poftquam eò productum fibi vitam vidit Ut filium vidret Anglie Cancellarium, fers in terra fe jam moratum ratus, libens emigravit in Cœlum—Alt Filius, d fundo Patre, cui quamdiu fuperevat, comparatus juvenis vocari confueverat . & iple quoque filio u liberat, amiffum jam patrem requirens, ac editos ex fe liberos quatuor, & nepotes undecem, refpiciens apud ammum fuum, capt infenefiere, auxit hinc affectum animi, fubfecuta fi tum ad petenti fenti faquam, Pectoris voletudo deterior It igus mortalium bonum rerum Satin quin tum à pittro nere femper cbt rerat ut ultimos ul quasi Vue fua annos obtinere liberos quibus huius vitae n ut... paula in fe feducens futuram poffe immortel tatem medi ut, quamvem tandem, (fi cœptis annuat Deus) in In'gensifimo Prin p s incomparabili beneficio, ufignatis honoribus imp tib requeue ho. Sepulchrum fib, qu l mortis cum nunquam ceffantis adhepere quotidie commonefieret, (tranflatis hic prioris uxor s oßibus) extruendum curavit Quod ne fuperft s frustrà fib fecerit, neve ingruentem trepidus mortem horreat, fed defiderio Cur ifti liberus opperat mortem, ut fibi non omnino moriens, fea j mu m vitae felicior s inveniat Precibus cum pus, Lector optime, fpernentem precor, defunctumque profequere.

Clara Thomae jacet hic Joanna Uxoriculi MORI,
Qui tumulum Alicie, huic deftino quique mihi
Una mihi dedit hoc conjunct i virentibus annis,
M recet ut puer & trini puelli patrem
Altera Privignis (quae Gloria rara Novercae eft)
Tam pia, quam natis vix fuit ulla fuis
Altera fic mecum vixit, fic altera vivt.
Charior, incer tum eft, quae fit, an illa fuit
O fimul, O junct i poteramus vivere nos tres
Quam bene, fi fatum Religioque finat
At facret Tumulus, facret nos, obfecro, Cœlum
Sic, mors non potuit quod dare vita, dabit.

In Englifh thus   In the Jear, 1532.

THomas Moore, born in the City of London, of a Family honeft, tho' not very famous, was yet very convenient with Letters Who after he had for fome Years, (when Young) pleaded feveral Caufes in the Hall and City, and been Judge in the Sheriff's Court, He was by the invincible K Henry VIII, (to whom only the unheard of Glory happened to be ftil'd Defender of the Faith, which he bravely deferved both by his Pen and Sword) fent for to Court, made one of the King's Council and Knighted ; firft, Vice-Treafurer, and then Chancellor of the Dutchy of Lancifter, and at length by the wonderful Favour of his Prince, made Chancellor of England But in the mean time he was chofen Speaker of the Houfe of Commons, and Embaffidor at feveral times to feveral Princes And laftly at Cambray, a Companion and Colleague, join'd with the Head of the Emb affy Cutb rt Tunftall, late B of London, and afterwards of Durham, (than which Lord, the World fees not this Day any Man more learned, prudent or virtuous) there amongft the chiefeft Monarchs of the Chriftian World, the League renewed, and much wifh'd for Peace reftor'd, he faw with Joy, and was in Embaffadour prefent at the Treaty

With Peace may Heaven continue in lafting make

And while he was employ'd in the Courfe of thefe Offices and Honours, fo that neither the beft of Princes could blame his labours, nor was he odious to the Nobility, nor offenfive to the People : Troublefome only to Thieves and Murderers His Father, Sir John Moore, Kt was advanc'd by the King to that Rank amongft the Judges, which is called, a Juftice of the King's Bench A Perfon in his Behaviour, civil, pleafant, innocent, mild, merciful, juft and upright, loaded with Years, but of a conftitution of Body above his Age After he had liv'd to fee his Son Chancellor of England judging that he had ftand long enough in this Life, willingly he travell'd to Heaven—but the Son after his Death (to whom compar'd when alive, he was call'd the young Man, and feem'd to be himfelf,) miffing his aldeft Father, and weighing in his Mind that he had Four Children and Eleven Grandchildren, begun to feem old, that ftate of Health, (the ftrength of approaching Death) following entered his Opinion Therefore being full and cloy'd with Temporal Affairs, That which from his Infancy he had pray'd for, that the latter Days of his Life might be free, that withdrawing himfelf from the hurry and bufinefs of the World, he might meditate on Immortality, to come (if God favour his Attempts) refigning all his Honours, he will beg to obtain by the incomparable Benefit of a most indulgent Prince - And this Monument he took care to be erected for himself, which should put him in mind of his Death, that approach'd and crept upon him every Day (having removed the Bones of his former Wife here) which while alive he should not in vain have done, nor like a Coward be afraid of Death the Assailant, but for the sake of Christ to seek the same, in order to find not altogether Death, but a Door to enter into a happier Life. Kind Reader, both living and dead, I beseech you to favour him with your pious Prayers.

> Sir *Thomas Moore's* first loving Wife lies here,
> I or *Alice* and my self this Tomb I rear
> By *Joan* I had Three Daughters and one Son,
> Before my prime of vig'rous Strength was gone
> To them such Love was by *Alice* shown,
> (In Step-mothers a Virtue rarely known,)
> The World believ'd the Children were her own
> Such is *Alice*, such *Joanna* was,
> It's hard to judge which was the happier Choice
> If Piety or Life our Prayers could grant
> To join us Three, we should no blessings want
> One Grave shall hold us, yet in Heaven well live,
> And Death grants that which Life could never give

This Great Man was Beheaded on Tower-hill 1532 for not taking the Oath of Supremacy,

Next the preceding Monument on the same side, is a neat Square Black Marble Stone, with the Arms of the Mareschal *De la Force*, and Sir *Theodore Mayern* quarter'd together, and on it the following Inscription in Letters of Gold

D O M S

Elizabethæ Eoutus Theodori de Moverne, Baronis Albinæ Filiæ, Petri D Gaumont Marchionis de Cugnac (Petre Henrico de Gaumont) Marchione de Castlemont, & Avo Jacobo nonpar de Gaumont, Duce de la Force, primo Franciæ Mareschall. Regiorum Exercituum longo Imperatore Fortissimo, Fortunatissimo, Invictissimo nati) Uxori dulcissimæ, Lectissimæ, charissimæ, Post nupt ac mense, acerbo eriptæ fato, Conjux in Amoris incontentis, & corrupta fides Monumentum mærens posuit.
Obiit X° Julii 1653 in Pago Chelsey, juxta Londinum Vixit annos XX, Menses VI,
Dies 3° Resurget

Σὺν Θεῷ.

This Monument is erected to the Memory of *Elizabeth*, Daughter of Sir *Theodore Mayern*, Kt. Baron of *Albon*, Wife of *Petro De Gaumont* Marquess of *Cugnac*, (Son of *Henry De Gaumont* Marquess *De Castlemont*, and Grandson to *James Nonpar De Gaumont*, Duke *Del Force*, first Mareschal of *France*, for many Years the most Valiant, Fortunate, and Invincible General of the Kings Armies) Her sorrowful Husband as a Proof of his unblacked Love and never violated Faith, to his most Dear beloved and highly approved Lady, snatch'd away by Cruel Death, 16 Months after her Marriage, has Dedicated this Monument.

She dyed the 10th of *July* 1653 in the Village of *Chelsea*, near *London*. She lived 20 Years 6 Months and 3 Days.

She will rise again with God.

This Lady here Interr'd was Married to the Marquess *De Cugnac*, (of a Protestant Family) Famous in the Reigns of *Henry* IV *Lewis* XIII and XIV This Noble man perceiving by the Intrigues of *Cardinal Richlieu*, and his Successor *Mazarine*, that the *Protestants* were to be expelled *France*, took Sanctuary here in *England*, and brought with him a Fortune Sufficient to support the Character which he bore in that Kingdom He had with her every considerable Estate, She being the only Daughter and Heir to Sir *Theodore Mayern*, Kt. Chief Physician to K *Charles* I (by whom he was Knighted,) and *Henrietta Maria* his Queen Sir *Theodore* lies Buried in the *Chancel* of St. *Martins* in the Fields She Dyed of the Small Pox The Rest may be learnt from the Monument.

An Antient Monument, having the Effigies of *Thomas Hawkins Esq*, and Three sons kneeling on one Side to Altar, and his Wife and Daughter on the other, upon it this Inscription

Here lies the Body of *James Hawkins* late of *Chelsea*, in the County of *Middlesex*, the Second Son of *Robert Hawkins* the Elder, of *Chelsea* in the County of *York* which both served King *Henry* VIII in the Room of a Gentleman Pensioner, and was with his Majesty at the winning of *Bologne*, and King *Edward* VI at *Muscleborough Hill*, I also Queen

Mary and Queen *Elizabeth* in their Affairs, being of the Age of Seventy Years, who had to Wife *Ursula Maidenhead*, the Daughter of the Lady *Sands*. *Anno Domini*, 1556.

Upon a Square white Marble Stone, the following Inscription.

HIC propè situm est Corpus
Doctissimi Viri & de literis optimè meritis
Adami Littleton. S T. P.
Capellani Regis Canonici
Westmonasteriensis
Hujus Ecclesiæ,
(Per spatium XXIV annorum) Rectoris
Omnibus hujus Parochiæ Incolis
Unicè chari :
I stirpe antiquâ & venerabili oriundi.
Obiit Ultimo die Junii 1694.
Anno ætatis suæ 67.

English'd thus.

NEAR this Place lies the Body
Of that most Learned
And most ingenuous Gentleman
Adam Littleton D. D
Prebendary of the Royal Cathedral
At *Westminster*
Rector of this Church
(For the space of XXIV Years.)
Entirely beloved
By the Gentry and Commons of this Parish.
He was Descended from an Antient
And Noble Family.
He dyed the last Day of *June* 1694.
On the 67th. Year of his Age.

This Gentleman was descended from a younger Branch of Sir *John Littleton*, Baron of *Mounslow*, sometime Lord Keeper of the Great Seal of *England*, in the Reign of K *Charles* I. whose Ancestor was Judge *Littleton*, in the Reign of King *Henry* IV (to whom we owe the great Knowledge of our Common Law) He was bred up at *Oxford*, and distinguish'd there for his Knowledge in the Oriental Tongues Whilst he was Canon of *Westminster*, he had a Grant from K *Charles* II to succeed Dr *Richard Busby* in the Mastership of that Great School ; for which he was highly qualified, his Latin Dictionary will perpetuate his Name to all Posterity

In the North Chancel, the North-East part of the Church.

An antient Monument neatly perform'd, having the Effigies of *Thomas Laurence*, Esq; (Father of Sir *John Laurence*) with his Three Sons, and *Eliz.* his Wife, with Six Daughters all Kneeling Underneath the following Lines

THE Years wherein I liv'd, were Fifty four,
October Twenty Eight did end my Life,
Children Eleven God left in store,
Sole Comfort of their Mother and my Wife
The World can say, what I have been before,
What I am now, Examples still are rife
Thus *Thomas Laurence* speaks to Times ensuing,
That Death is sure, and Time is past renewing

A Plain Monument of black Marble fixt against the Wall, having Two Dorick Pillars, and a Coat of Arms Upon it is follows,

Sacred to the Memory
OF Sir *John Laurence* late of Iver
In the County of *Bucks*, Knight and Barronet,
Who married *Griffel* the Daughter
Of *Edmund Gibbs* of *Kent* Esq, by whom
He had Nine Seven Sons and Four Daughters,
He dyed the Thirteenth of *November*, 1638.
Aged Fifty Years.

When

When Bad Men Dye, and turn to their laft Sleep,
What Stir the Poets and Engravers keep ,
Try a feign'd Skill to pile them up a Name,
With Terms of Good and Juft out-lafting Fame,
Alas' Poor Men, fuch have moft need of Stone,
And Epitaphs ; the good indeed lack none,
Their own true Worth's enough to give of Glory,
Unto their Names, which will Survive all Story
Such was the Man lies here, who doth partake,
Of Verfe and Stone, but 'tis for Fafhion's fake

Near the laft, is a Monument very remarkable and furprizing, being the Reprefentation
of a Woman about the bignefs of the Life, as rifing from the Dead on the laft Day
She is upon her Knees, with Eyes and Hands lift up towards Heaven , fronting
the Body of the Church, and has her winding Sheet wrapt round her The whole
Performance being of Marble, is an extraordinary Piece of Workmanfhip.

Underneath is a large Infcription in Letters of Gold as followeth

AND you fhall know, that I am the Lord, when I have opened your Graves, and brought
you up, O my People, out of the Deep, *Ezek* 37 Chap V 12
SACRED
To the Bleffed Memory, of that
Unftain'd Copy and rare Example
Of all Virtue,
S A R A H ,
Wife to *Richard Calvis* of *Newton*,
In the Ifle of *Ely* in the County
of *Cambridge Efq*,
the Daughter of *Thomas Lawrence* of *Iver*
In the County of *Bucks*, who in the Fortieth Year
Of her Age received a Glorious reward
Of her Conftant Piety,
Being the Happy Mother of 8 Sons and 2 Daughters

Wonder not, Reader, how this Stone,
Shou'd be fo fmooth and pure, there s one
That lies within, by whofe fair Light,
It fhines fo clear and looks fo Bright
The Carver's Art cou'd only give
A Form, but not the Power to live
Nor fhall it ever loofe its Grace,
Till fhe arife, and have the Place .
For lofs of whom the mournful Urn
Shall Live, and to Cinders turn
Obiit 17 Apr 1631.

In this Chancel lie two large Black Marble Stones, under which are interr'd the Bodies
of Dame *Griffell*, Wife of Sir *John Lawrence*, and *Henry Lawrence*, Turky Merchant their Son

Between the Two Chancels is a ftately Monument, rais'd in form of an Arch, hollow,
and open at both ends, embellifh'd with Rofes, Branches, and other Antique Works

Upon one fide is Written
Richards, Rector, Gervafis funera cernis,
Und hic parte fua corpore nempe caret
Juris Confulus, Jus mortis non fugit atque,
Jus habet in Juvenes, jus habet in q, Jene.
Omnes illa rapit, nullo difcrimine fervat,
Sevris aut citius, Blanda truculenta venit ,
Illa furens juvenis juventilia fila refoluit
Annis at Juvenis, Maxue erat ifte fevex
Hunc fuper oftia tulit fragilis inconftantis vita
Eximit e Terris Religionis Amor.

In Inglifh
The Tomb of *Richard Fervioufe*, Reader, view
One part of him, his Body now he wants

The

The Laws of Death the Lawyer cannot break;
O'er Old and Young he claims a legal Power
Sooner or later cruel Death appears,
And Rich and Poor without diftinction takes.
Raging he cuts too foon his Thread of Life,
In Years though young, in Underftanding old.
The Love of Piety from Earth him bears,
And Life's inconftant State fends him to Heaven.

A Black Marble Stone in the Wall, adjoining to the Monument of the Lady *Cheyne*.

Here Underneath

Lieth what was Mortal of *James Buck*, Efq, who departed this Life, *December* 21ft. in his Climacterical, (to wit) in the 63d Year of his Age. He was Son to *Matthew Buck* of *Winterburne*, in the County of *Glocefter*, Efq, by *Mary* his Wife, Daughter of Sir *Peter Buck*, of *Rochefter* in the County of *Kent*, Kt He had to Wife, *Elizabeth*, Daughter of *Humphrey Rogers*, of *Richmond*, in the County of *Surry*, Efq, He had Iffue, Five Sons and one Daughter, *James, Francis, Elizabeth, Charles, John* and *Richard*, whereof the Four firft are ftill furviving His Wife *Elizabeth* having lived 20 Years married, died *Nov.* 23d 1674 in the 50th Year of her Age, and lies buried in *Barkhamfted* Church in *Hertfordfhire*, with her Anceftors.

About the middle of the North-fide of the Church againft the Wall, is a ftately Monument, a moft exquifite Piece of Workmanfhip (exceeding moft of the modern Performances in the Abby of *Weftminfter*,) the whole is rais'd about 14 Feet from the Ground, and is of grey Marble, the Architrave, *&c* at top fupported by 2 neat Corinthian Pillars of the fame Stone Within is a large Nitch, in which the Lady *Jane Cheyne* is reprefented in white Marble, as big as the Life, lying upon her right fide, leaning upon a Bible : Behind her in Letters of Gold, as alfo upon its Bafe, is the following Infcription handfomely done. This Monument was done by the famous *Seignior Bernini* an Italian, and coft 500 *l*.

M. S.

Plentiffimæ & Sanctiffimæ Heroinæ
    Nec tàm avitis Imaginibus quam propter
            Virtutes illuftris,
        Dominæ *Janæ Cheynæ*.
Excellentiffimi Domini Gulielmi Ducis de Novo Caftro,
        Filiæ ex tribus natu maximæ,
            Caroli Cheynæ Armigeri,
    Conjugis dilectiffimæ, defideratiffimæ
De quá nihil unquam doluit, nifi de Morte ;
Ex quá tres optimè fpes liberos fufcepit,
        Elizabetham & Gulielmum,
    Et Venuftam Deo Catharinam,
Intra paucos à Morte matris menfes
            Fato functam.
    Inter cætera Charitatis Opera,
        Tectum huic Ecclefiæ,
Denfis trabibus Ordinibus compingendum,
    (Quod jam Dei gratiâ effectum eft)
Paulò ante mortem tanquam ex Legato debitum,
Vitæ curriculum, quâ Pietate & Patientiâ
Tranfegerat, peregit, pridiè Idus Octobris
        ⎰ Salutis. MDCLXIX
Anno ⎱   Ætatis 48
        ⎰ Et Conjugis XV.
Toto propè tempore hanc parochiam
            Nobilitavit, Bravit.
    Jacet und eum Filiolâ Catharinâ,
Inter Cancellos in medio conditorio Sepulta
        Sub ipfa facrâ Menfâ.

Under-

Underneath the Figure of the Lady *Jane*, on a black Oval Marble Stone, is this Inscription

M.   S.

Caroli Cheyne
Vicecomitis de Newhaven in Regno Scotiæ
Hujus Mannerii de Chelsey Domini
Qui hoc Monumentum in memoriam
Dominæ Janæ Uxoris primæ
Dilectissimæ annos abhinc viginti novem
Extruxerat   ac nunc demum ipse
(Heu nimium cito) demortuus
Et juxta conjugem suam (prout testamento
Suo designaverat) in eodem Conditorio
Sepultus una cum illa beatam resurrectionem
Præstolatur Obiit 30 die Junii
Anno { *Domini* 1698
       { *Ætatis* 74

At the Foot of the Chancel, being the Entrance into the Vault of the Family, on a black Marble Stone is thus written.

In Sepulturam.

Lectissimæ Fæminæ
Conjugis suæ dilectissimæ
Pientissimæ Heroinæ Dominæ Janæ,
Excellentissimi Domini Gulielmi Ducis de Novo Castro,
Filiæ natu maximæ
Fato non ita pridem functi.
Suumque pariter ipsius & lucrum,
(Quam mortem oppetierint)
Subterraneum isthuc cinerum conditorium
Carolus Cheyne Armiger
Hujusce Manerii de Chelsey
(Cui emendo Dos ampla conjugis subsidium præbuit)
Dominus
Extruendum curavit
Et die tertio Kalendarum Novembris
Anni Salutis, 1669,
M.   L.   Sacravit
Faxit, oro, Deus optime, maxime
Ut quietè perfruatur hæc sepeliendi
Donec omnis Caro resurgat
Amen   Amen

In English.

Sacred to the Memory
Of the most Religious and Holy Heroine,
Not so famous for her ancient Nobility
As for her Virtues,
The Lady *Jane Cheyne,*
Eldest of Three Daughters,
Of the most excellent Prince *William,* Duke of *Newcastle*
The most dear and beloved Wife
Of *Charles Cheyne,* Esq;
Who was never offensive to him, but by Death ;
By whom he had 3 Children of great hopes,
Elizabeth and *William,*
And dear to Heaven, *Catharine,*
Who dyed
Some few Months after her Mother
Among many Works of Charity,
The Cieling of this Church,
With all the Beams, just before her Death
She bequeath'd as her last Legacy

(Which

(Which by the Grace of God is now finish'd)
The Course of this Life, which with Piety and Patience
She run through was finish'd,
The Day before the Ides of *October*.
of our Lord MDCLXIX
In the Year of her Age XLVIII.
and of her Marriage XV
For the greatest part of her time, this Parish
She Honour'd and made happy
She lies buried with her Daughter *Catharine*.

Between the two Chancels under the Communion Table

Sacred to the Memory
Of *Charles Cheyne*
VIscount *Newhaven* in the Kingdom of *Scotland*,
Lord of this Mannor of *Chelsea*
Who built this Monument to the Memory
Of the Lady *Jane* his first Wife
Who dyed 29 Years since, and now
He himself (Alas! too soon) is dead
(As he order'd by his last Will)
He lies buried in the same Vault,
With whom he expects a blessed Resurrection.
He departed this Life the 30th of *June*
In the Year { of our Lord, 1698
{ of his Age, 74.

On the Sepulchre.
Of that most extraordinary Lady,
His most beloved Wife,
That most pious Heroine the Lady *Jane*
Eldest Daughter
Of the illustrious Prince *William* Duke of *Newcastle*,
Not long since Deceas'd
In this Subterraneous Repository of Ashes
(When Death invades them)
Charles Cheyne, Esq,
Lord of this Mannor of *Chelsea*,
(Which was purchas'd by the rich Dowry of his Wife)
His and their Reliques
Took care shou'd be deposited
And made this Vault the third of the Kalends of *November*,
In the Year of our Lord, 1699

This noble Lord had for his second Wife (who now lives) the Widow of *John*, E of *Radnor*, he was descended from several eminent Persons, who have been Kts of the Garter, and Barons of this Realm. *William*, the present Lord *Cheyne*, only Son of these Two incomparable Persons, (who has been several times Kt of the Shire, for the County of *Bucks*,) inherits not only their large Fortunes, but also their singular Virtues.

Upon a black Marble Stone these words
THE Return of *Baldwin Howley*, Dr of Physick,
On the 14th of *May*, being *Whitsunday*,
In the Year of our Lord, 1676.
In the 70th Year of his Age

Near the South East Corner of the Church, stands a noble Monument of white Marble, (the Sight of part whereof is unhappily intercepted by a Gallery lately erected) having 2 large Figures as big as the Life standing, representing Justice and Fortitude, supporting the Arms of the *Stanleys* and 3 Vases In the middle is an Effigies of Sir *Robert Stanley* at half length,

And underneath this Inscription.

TO the last Memory
Of the truly Honourable Sir *Robert Stanley*,
Of the Noble Order of *Bath*

And Second Son of the **Right** Honourable
William Earl of *Derby*,
Who departed this Life the Third of *June*, 1632

This Noble Gentleman was one of the first Knights of this Order, Instituted by King *James* I in Honor of the Union of the Two Kingdoms. His Nephew, the Valiant and Heroick *James Earl* of *Derby*, was Beheaded for his Loyalty by the Parliament Faction in the Civil Wars.

A Noble Ancient Monument (cover'd by the said Gallery,) erected for the Lady *Jane Guilford* Dutchess of *Northumberland*, on which is represented, in Brass Plates, her Effigies, with all her Daughters and Sons, (to wit) *Mary*, *Margaret*, *Katherine*, *Francis*, and *Temperance*, and *Henry*, *Thomas*, *John*, *Ambrose*, *Robert*, *Guilford*, *Henry*, and *Charles*, and on it is this Inscription.

> Here lyeth interred the Right Noble and Excellent Princefs Lady *Jane Guilford*, late Dutchefs of *Northumberland*. Daughter and fole Heir of the Right Honourable Sir *Edward Guilford* Knight, Lord Warden of the 5 Ports. The which Sir *Edward* was Son to the Right Honourable Sir *Richard Guilford*, fometime Knight and Companion of the moft Noble Order of the Garter, and the faid Dutchefs was Wife to the High and Mighty Prince *John Dudley* late Duke of *Northumberland*, by whom fhe had Iffue Eight Sons and Five Daughters, and after fhe had lived Forty Six Years, fhe departed this tranfitory World at her Manner of *Chelfea*, the Twenty Second Day of *January*, in the Second Year of the Reign of our Sovereign Lady Mary I and in the Year 1555. On whofe Soul Jefus have Mercy.

This Lady *Jane* was Married to the Greateft Subject of that Age, *John Dudley* Duke of *Northumberland*, whom fhe furvived Two Years. She lived to fee her Hufband, and *John* Lord of *Warwick* her Eldeft Son; both to be Condemned for High Treafon, the firft was Executed *August* 22, 1553 on *Tower-hill*, and the Son foon after dyed in Prifon. Her Sixth Son *Guilford*, (who fometime before was Married to the Lady *Jane Grey*,) the Ornament of Modefty, Learning, and Religion, was with his faid Wife alfo beheaded the 12 of *February*, 1554. Yet their Forth Son *Ambrofe*, came afterwards to be Earl of *Warwick*, Knight of the Garter, and Privy Counfellor to Queen *Elizabeth*. *Robert* the Fifth Son was the great Earl of *Leicefter*, Knight of the Order of the Garter, and St *Michael*, who excelled his Father in the Management of Affairs of State, and kept his Reputation to the laft, with his moft Gracious Queen *Mary* her Fifeft Daughter was Married to Sir *Henry Sidney* Knight of the Garter, and feveral times Lord Lieutenant of *Ireland*, by whom fhe had Sir *Philip Sidney*, (the moft Accomplifh'd Gentleman in *Europe*,) and *Robert* from whom in a direct Line is defcended *Robert*, the prefent Earl of *Leicefter*. Its Obfervable, that though this Lady had Eight Sons, (who were all Perfons of Comely Shape and Appearance,) yet none of them had ever any lawful Iffue.

A Monument rais'd about Four Foot from the Ground, with the Effigies of Sir *Arthur Gorges*, his Lady, Three Sons and Five Daughters, in Brafs Plates fixe thereon, and this Inscription.

In Obitum. Illuftrifsimi Viri Domini Arthuri Gorges Equitis Zmato Epicedium

Englifh'd thus

THE deflent, nati, natæ, celeberrime conjux, *Te dolet angufta m efta Catervæ Schola. Aft Lucemus air, fe vivo, non periturum Arthinum Congeis, transfuit ipfe Deus, Arthuras cupiens Arthurus adire per annos, Et Novus es ejus Nomine vivus adeft*	FOR thee, Dear Sir, thy Sons and Daughter Weep, For thee, the learned Iule Lament and Mourn, But Live in Blifs, He living, you cant Dye, Its God alone tranflates you to the Sky, Whilft *Arthur* flies to the Ætherial Seats, He worthy Son makes great his Noble Name

Near the laft is a Neat Monument of black and white Marble, and thefe Lines.

> Here lies interr'd the Body of that Generous, and Worthy Gentleman, *John Gorges* Efq; Eldeft Son of Sir *Arthur Gorges* Knight, the laft furviving Branch of that Honourable Family, Who departed this Life, the Eighth of *April*, 1668.
>
> He Married Dame *Mary*, one of the Daughters, and Coheirs of *Paul Vifcount Banning*. She firft Married to *William* Lord *Grandifon*, afterwards to *Charles* Lord of *Inghifn*, and Thirdly to the faid deceafed *Arthur Gorges*, whom fhe furvived, and departed this Life, and lyes here Buried with her loving Husband, to whofe, and to her own Memory, fhe erected this Tomb.

HEre Sleeps, and Feels no Preſſure of the Stone,
He that had all the Gorges Souls in one,
Here the Ingenious Valiant ARTHUR lies,
To be bewail'd by Marble, and Our Eyes,
By moſt beloved, but love cannot retrieve
Dead Friends, has Power to Kill, not to relieve
Let him reſt free from Cares, and Toilſome Pain,
When all the GORGES riſe, he'll riſe again.
This laſt retiring Room, his own doth call,
Who after Death, has that, and Heaven has all !
Live Arthur by the Spirit of thy Fame,
Chelſea it ſelf muſt Dye, before thy Name.

This Worthy Gentleman was very Converſant with the late Duke of Buckingham, the Earl of Rochſter, and the Celebrated Wits of that time He Tranſlated ſeveral Parts of Lucan, and a Volume of his Poetry is now extant, very much eſteem'd by the learned World.

On the South Side of the Church, is a moſt ſtately Monument of white Marble, (ſecur'd with Iron Rails.) The Architrave at Top ſupported by Two Corinthian Pillars, with the Cumbent Effigies of George and Anne, Barons of Dacre, as big as the Life On each ſide is a lofty Pyramid, and the whole is Embelliſh'd with curious Pieces of Flowers, neatly In-laid and ſeveral Elaborate Pieces of Moſaick Work.

Engliſh'd thus

In Obitum Nobiliſſimorum Conjugum, Georgii Domini Dacres, & Annæ Uxoris.	On the Death of that moſt Noble Peer, George Baron Dacres, and Anne his Wife

QUos Ardens copulavit Amor Juvenilibus Annis, Abſtulit atra Dies, mors inopina rapit. Ille Prior fatis Dacrorum Nobile Germen Occidit, in Morbum aſt incidit illa prius. Quæ Langueſcendo miſeræ præ tædia Vitæ Senſit, tam dulci Conjuge caſſa ſuo : Ut Teneri cordis Concordia Junxerat ambos. Sic Idem amborum conteget oſſa Locus. Quos jungit Tumulus, conjungent Cælica Tecta. Ut Teneant Cælum, qui tenuere fidem.	Whom in their tender Years true Love has joyn'd, Remorſeleſs Death at length has Snatch'd away, She firſt fell Sick, but this moſt Noble Lord, The laſt of Dacres Race too ſoon expir'd, She languiſhing and pining for her Love, Cou'd not ſurvive ſo ſenſible a Loſs As one true Love, theſe Two alone did bleſs, See the ſame Tomb ſhall cover both their Bones, As in the Grave, ſo they in Heaven will Joyn A Juſt Reward for their unſpotted Faith.

Nobilis iſta Vir obiit. 25 Decemb. 1594	Nobilis iſta Mulier obiit. 14 Maii, 1595	This Noble Lord died, 25 Decem. 1594	This Noble Lady died, 14 of May, 1595

This Noble Lord was the laſt Baron Dacres of Giſland, in the County of Cumberland, which had Flouriſh'd in this Kingdom for near Three Hundred Years The Lady Anne his Wife is famous for Erecting Almes Houſes for Ten Old-men, and Ten Old-women near Tuttle Fields, who are allowed 16 l per Annum, each of them for ever, the Lord Mayor and Aldermen for the time being, are by her laſt will and Teſtament, made the Truſtees of this her Charity

Without the Church, on the New additional Brick Building, at the Southweſt Corner of the Church, upon a large Stone fixt againſt the Wall about Eight Foot long, and Three over, having an Urn at Top, is this Inſcription

1 7 0 3. Poſteritati ſacrum, More Majorum, Extrà urbis Pomæria, Juxtà Viam Publicam In Tumulo edittore, Heu Propè imhumari Voluit, Edvardus Chamberlayne, Anglus, Chriſticola, I. D Ex antiquâ Comitis Tanquervillæ Proſapiâ Normannica Oriundus, Oddingtoniæ Natus, 1616. Gloceſtriæ Grammatica, Oxonii Juriſprudentia, Londini Humanitate Imbutus fuit.	1 7 0 3. Sacred to Poſterity, In Imitation of our Anceſtors, Without the Walls of the City, And near the High Way In an Elevated Tomb By this Place would be Buried, Edward Chamberlayne, An Engliſhman, Chriſtian, and Doctor of Laws, Deſcended from the Ancient Norman Race of the Earl of Tanquerville, Born at Oddington, 1616. He learnt Grammar at Gloceſter, The Civil Law at Oxon, And Humanity at London.

Per Galliam, Hispaniam, Italiam, Hungariam,	He travell'd through France, Spain,
Bohemiam, Utramque Germaniam, Daniam,	Italy, Hungary, Bohemia, both
& Sueciam Migravit.	Germany's, Denmark, and Sweden
Susannam Clifford Equestri Familia prognatam	He Married in 1658
In Matrimonium duxit, 1658	*Susanna Clifford* sprung from a Knightly Family
Novem Liberos genuit, Sex Libros composuit.	He had Seven Children, and made 6 Books
Tandem 1703. *in terram Oblivionis*	At length he Travell'd in 1703
Semigravit	Into the Land of Oblivion
Benefaciendis Universis, etiam & Posteris	He was so studious to do good to all Men,
Adeo studiosus fuit, ut secum condi	And especially to Posterity ;
Jusserat i bres aliquot suos cerâ obvolutos,	That he Order'd some of his Books
Seris forsan postritati aliquando profuturos.	Cover'd with Wax to be Buried with him,
	Which may be of use to times to come
Abi Viator, fac simile	God preserve thee, O Traveller '
Deus te servet Incolumem,	Be gone, and Imitate him.
Hoc Monumentum	This Monument
Non Impunè temerandum	By no means to be violated
In Honoris juxta ac maeroris testamentum	*Walter Harris* Doctor of Physick,
Pont curavit	(A Friend for a Friend,)
Gualterus Harris,	As a Testimony both of his respect and Grief,
M D	Took care should be erected
Amicus Amico.	

The abovenam'd Doctor *Edward Chamberlayne*, hath settled for ever a rent Charge of 5 *l.* a Year, to Bind a Poor Boy in *Chelsea*, to a Waterman of *Chelsea*

Near the last is a Plain Marble Stone about Eighteen Inches Broad, and Three Foot long, and on it as followeth

Posteritati Sacrum.	Sacred to Posterity.
HIC *Juxta Situs est Peregrinus Clifford*	NEar this Place lyes interr'd
Chamberlayne, Dux Marinus, Filius Natu	*Peregrine Clifford* Chamberlayne,
Maximus Edvardi Chamberlayne,	A Sea-Captain,
L D	Eldest Son of Sir *Edward Chamberlayne*
Natus fuit Hagæ Comit 1, 1660	Doctor of Laws.
Qui tum Linguis, Scientiis Liberalibus,	Born at the Hague, 1660
Studio Legum Municipalum, Artibus	Who gave himself to the Study
Pingendi, Psallendi, Digladiandi, Modulandi,	Of Languages, and Liberal Sciences,
Terras, & regiones dimetiendi,	And of the Municipal Laws,
Sed præ Omnibus operam Navigandi did sit,	To the Arts of Painting, Singing, Fencing,
Quatuor Mundi plag is lustrâsset,	Surveying, and the Mathematiques.
Regi & Patriæ fidel ter ac strenuè contra	But above all things to Navigation
Gallos & Indos meruisst, h n' Præmaturè	He view'd the Four parts of the World,
In terra: Oblivionis semigravit,	And after he had deserv'd well,
Sexto, Novembris, 1691	Both of his King and Country, (*Indians* ;
	For Fighting Valiantly against the *French* and
Hoc Monumentum non Impunè	He too soon Travell'd to the Land of Oblivion,
Temerandum Post curavit	The Sixth of November, 1691.
Mœrens Pater	This Monument not without Punishment to be
	His sorrowful Father [disturb'd.
	Took care should be erected.

Over the South Door is a Marble Stone about Five Foot long, and Eight Inches Broad, with these Lines

HIC *Juxta in Conditorio Depositus Edvi l*	NEar this Place in a Vault is Buried *Edward*
dus Chamberlayne, filius natu minimus	*Chamberlayne,* youngest Son of *Edward*
Edvardi Chamberlayne L D Qui in Schola	*Chamberlayne* Doctor of Laws, who was first
Westmonasteriensi, Postea in Collema Oxo-	brought up in *Westminster* School, afterwards
mensi, Deinde in Collegio Templi interioris	in the University of *Oxford,* and lastly, in the
Londinensis Educatus, tandem pro Rege &	Inner Temple, *London* At length he deserv'd
Patria contra Gallos per Mare navers Meluit,	well at Sea from his King and Country against
ubi per Septennium Littus apud Marinorum,	the French, who after Seven Years service be-
tum demum facial. Plumirde mist Quatriduum	ing seiz'd by a fatal Plumbie, he dyed in Four
abreptus fuit, optimæ Spei juvenis, Natus Nono	days A Young Gentleman of great hopes, He
Calendarum Octobris, 1669 *Denatus Pridie*	was Born the 9th of the Calends of Oct 1669,
Idus Maii, 1698.	and dyed the day before the Ides of May 1698
	This Monument (not justly to be disturb'd
Hoc Monumentum non impunè temerandum	without Punishment) his sorrowful other took
Pont curavit Mœrens Pa r	care to be Erected The

The following Monument is the same in form and size, as her Brother Peregrine *Clifford Chamberlayne's.*

HIC *juxtà in Conditorio Jacet Anna,*
Edvardi Chamberlayne
L. D.
Filia Unica
Londini *Nata,* 20th Januarii, 1667.
Quæ diù spreto connubio, Magnaque
Supra Sexum & ætatem Moliens,
30th Junii, 1690
Contra francigenas Armis, habituque Virilis
In Rate flammiferà Sex horas sub duce fratre
Pugnavit, Dum virgo fuit , Dum casta Virago
Heroum poterat Stirpem generare Masinam
Ni præmaturis fatis abrepta fuisset .

Redux ab istà navali Pugnà ,
Ac post aliquot Menses Nupta
Johan. Spragg *Armigero,*
Quicum vixit amantissime Sesquiannum
Tandem enixa filiam post paucos dies
Obiit 30th Octobris, 1691
Hoc Monumentum
Uxori Charissimæ
Nec non Pudicissimæ
Poni curavit Maritus

NEar this Place in a Vault lies *Anne*
Onely Daughter,
Of *Edward Chamberlayne* Doctor of Laws
Born at *London,* the 20th. of *January,* 1667.
Who for a long time slighting Marriage,
And attempting great things
Above her Age and Sex;
On the 30th of *June,* 1690
Cloath'd like a Man on Board a Fire Ship,
Six Hours against the French she bravely Fought,
(Her Brother being Captain,) too soon, alass !
by Cruel Death to Heaven she is Convey'd,
Before she had brought forth a Marine Heroe
Returning from this Sea Fight,
After some few Months
She was Married to *John Spragg* Esq,
With whom she most lovingly lived
For a Year and a Half ,
At length few Days after being brought to Bed
Of a Daughter, she dyed the 30 of *Octob* 1691.
This Monument
Her sorrowful Husband
For his most beloved, and most virtuous Wife
Took care shou'd be Erected

Another large Stone much like the Doctor's, standing on the other Side the Window and on it thus.

NEar this Place
In a Vault belonging to the Family,
Lies interr'd the Body of
SUSANNAH CHAMBERLAYNE,
Late Widow of Doctor *Edward Chamberlayne,*
And only Daughter of *Richard Clifford* Esq,
Descended from the Ancient
And Noble Family of the *Cliffords ,*
Lords of *Frampton*
In the County of *Glocester*
Aged Sixty Nine Years, and Three Months
She Dyed the 17th of *December*
In the Year of our Lord, 1703

These Monuments sufficiently display this Family, what remains to be observ'd is only that the said Doctor, (Author of that Useful Book the Present State of England,) had the Honour to be Preceptor to his Royal Highness the Prince, for the English Tongue, and has left behind him only one Son *John Chamberlayne* Esq, a Gentleman of the Princess Bed Chamber, one of her Majesties Justices of the Peace for the County of *Middlesex,* and F R S

These are the Monuments of this small Church, which if consider'd in their Number, Structure, or Dignity, are scarce to be parallel'd by any Parish Church of its bigness in *England* 'Tis probable, there might be many more formerly in the Pavement, but these were either torn up, 'tis like, in the late Rebellion, for the Value of their Brass, (as was too usual) or else defac'd in New Paving the Church, there being nothing now left that seems Ancient There are many more Monuments, in and about this Church of lesser Note, which we thought not proper to take notice of, having we fear been too particular already

Of the Advowson

The Right of Presentation to this Living, is in the Right Honourable *William* Lord
Ch Viscount *Newhaven* in the Kingdom of *Scotland,* and Lord of this Mannor
The Rectory of *Chelsea* is valued in the Queens Book but is said to
be th, as now improv'd above 300 *l per Annum* The Worthy and Reverend Dr. *John King*
Rector This

This Church fituated about the Center of the Parifh, ſtands about Two Meaſur'd Miles from *Charing-croſs*, and its Parifh extends it ſelf from a ſmall Creek, which runs under *Bloody-bridge*, and ſeparates it from St *Martins* in the Fields towards the Eaſt, to another ſmall Creek at *Sand-end*, which parts it from *Fulham* towards the Weſt, in all near a Mile, towards the North it borders upon *Kenſington*, and its Southern Shore is Waſh'd by the River *Thames*

The TOWN

THis Town according to *Camden* received its Name *Cheſſey* or *Snelſiey*, from a Bed of Sand near it in the River *Thames*, but being in Ancient Records call'd *Chelche-hith*, (which has no ſuch Signification,) we believe that Opinion only Conjectural   The Situation of it upon the Thames (as before) is very Pleaſant, and ſtanding in a ſmall Bay, or Angle, made by the meeting of *Chelſea* and *Batterſea* Reaches, it has a moſt delightful Proſpect on that River for near Four Miles, (to wit) is far as *Vaux-hall* Laſtward, and *Wanſworth* towards the Weſt

The greateſt part of the Buildings lie ſtretch'd along by the *Thames* ſide, and (with the Royal Hoſpital) at ſome diſtance make a pleaſant Proſpect   The Body of the Town is near the Church, from whence come Two Rows of Buildings, a conſiderable Way toward the North call'd *Church-lane*, toward the Weſt likewiſe are Buildings on both ſides the way to the Duke of *Beauforts*, and beyond there are many ſcatter'd Houſes and good Seats   At the Laſt End of the Town Runs a Street up from the *Thames* as far as the Royal Hoſpital, and beyond it a Row of Houſes a conſiderable way towards *London*   This Town was ever much reſorted to by Perſons of good Faſhion, and *Camden* ſays, was Beautified with ſeveral ſtately Piles by *Henry* VIII and *William Pawlet* Marquels of *Wincheſter*, Sir *Thomas Moore* Lord Chancellor of *England* had likewiſe a Seat here, where he was often Honour'd with the Viſits of his Royal Maſter, but the remains of thoſe Buildings are ſcarcely now to be ſeen, but that which will for ever render this Place Famous, and make it's Name out-laſt Time, is, that 'twas here, the Renown'd Princeſs *Elizabeth* (afterwards Queen) was Nurſt, part of the Nurſery yet remaining, which with ſeveral New Additional Buildings, is the Manſion-Houſe of the Lord *Cheyne* Lord of this Mannor

The Sweetneſs of its Air, and Pleaſant Situation, has of late Years drawn ſeveral Eminent Perſons to reſide and Build here, and fill'd it with many Worthy Families of Gentry, Citizens, and others, alſo the Schools with a great Number of Boarders, eſpecially Young Ladies, and it has Flouriſh'd ſo extreamly for Twenty or Thirty Years laſt paſt, that from a ſmall ſtragling Village, 'tis now become a large Beautiful and Populous Town, having about Three Hundred Houſes, and above that Number of Families, ſome of which are very great, (which is near Nine times its Number in the Year 1664

Its Vicinity to *London* no doubt has been no ſmall Cauſe of its late prodigious Growth, and indeed 'tis not much to be wondered why a Place ſhould ſo Flouriſh, where a Man may perfectly enjoy the Pleaſures of Country and City together, and when he Pleaſes in leſs than an Hours time either by Water, Coach, or otherwiſe, be at the Court, *Exchange*, or in the midſt of his Buſineſs   The Walk to Town is very even and very Pleaſant

What we mean by the Pleaſures of the City here, is the good Converſation for which this Place is at Preſent noted, the many Honourable Worthy Inhabitants, being not more remarkable for their Titles, Eſtates, Employments, or Abilities, than for their Extraordinary Civility, and Condeſcention, and their kind and facetious Tempers, living in a perfect Amity among themſelves, and have a general meeting every Day at a Coffee-houſe near the Church, well known for the pretty Collection of Rarities in Nature and Art, ſome of which are very curious

This Happy ſpot is likewiſe bleſt by Nature, with a peculiar kind Soil, which produceth Nine or Ten rare Phyſical Plants not found elſewhere in *England*, and the Apothecary's Garden here, lying upon the Thames ſide, is a cleer Inſtance of the Opinion of the Learned *Botaniſts* of their Society, had of the Aptitude of the Soil for the Nouriſhment of the moſt Curious Plants   It being ſo near *London*, we forbear giving any further Account of it   That Ingenious Botaniſt Mr *Samuel Doody*, is appointed by the Apothecaries of *London* to have the Care and Management of it

Additions to Camden p 33) 3,6

Of the Seats and Conſiderable Inhabitants in this Pariſh

I. The firſt which deſerves our Notice is the ROYAL HOSPITAL, a Structure becoming the Bounty of its Royal Founders and Finiſhers, deſign'd for the Entertainment of Diſabled and Superannuated Soldiers   'Tis ſituated at the Laſt end of the Town, a convenient Diſtance from the *Thames*, and built of Brick corner'd with Stone, conſiſting of Two Wings, each 360 Feet long, near 80 Broad, and 3 Stories high, which are joyn'd together towards the North, by a Chappel and Hall, of near the ſame dimenſions, and lies open towards the South, having a Pleaſant view of the Gardens adjoyning, the *Thames* and part of *Surrey*   The Two Wings are divided into Sixteen Wards, which are conveniently contriv'd for the Accommodation of above 400 Men   The whole Houſe is oblig'd to attend Prayers in the Chappel twice every Day, to which belongs Two Chaplains, *viz.* the Reverend Doctor *Langthorn*, and Mr. *Hare*, there is in It an Organ, and extraordinary Rich Furniture of Plate, &c. given by the late King James, and fine Performances in Carving and Fretwork. They Dine and Sup every Day in the Hall in great Order, having a plentiful Allowance, at the upper end whereof is a separate Table for the Officers of the House, and over Head a Noble Painting, of King Charles II on Horseback, with several others as big as the Life, Design'd by Senior Virtu, Finish'd by Mr. Cook, the Gift of the Earl of Ranelaugh. The Pavement of both Chapel and Hall is of black and white Marble, and upon the Cornice of the Piazza towards the South, is this Inscription IN SUBSIDIUM ET LEVAMEN EMERITORUM SENIO BELLO-QUE FRACTORUM CONDIDIT CAROLUS SECUNDUS, AUXIT JACOBUS SE-CUNDUS, PERFECERE GULIELMUS ET MARIA REX ET REGINA, MDCXC. In the Middle of the Quadrangle form'd by the Building, is a Brass Statue of King Charles II. In the Ancient Roman Dress, somewhat bigger than the Life, standing upon a Marble Pedestal, Rail'd Round with Iron, given by Mr Tobias Ruslat, and cost 500 l. There are several Handsome Buildings adjoyning, which make Two other large Courts, and are the Apartments of the Officers and Servants of the House, the Lodgings and Hall of the Light Horse, the Infirmary and other necessary Offices. Behind the Buildings is a large piece of Ground Inclos'd, Planted and made into Walks for the Diversion of the Soldiers, and before is very good Gardens, and Canals running down to the Thames side. The whole takes up above Forty Acres of Ground, and was Design'd by Sir Christopher Wren, the Charge of its Building and Finishing, is Computed at above 150000 l. And it stands her Majesty in about 14000 l per Annum, for its Yearly Maintenance. There is now in it near Five Hundred Men, which with the Officers and Servants of the House, and out Pensioners, make near Eight Hundred. 'Tis Govern'd by a Governour, and Lieutenant Governour, who are the Honourable Colonel Hales and Commissary Crawford. There are likewise Five Commissioners appointed to take Care of it, who are the Right Honourable John Hou Esq, The Honourable ---- Bridges Esq, Sir Christopher Wren Kt and the Governour and Lieutenant Governour, 'Tis call'd a Garrison, and all the Members of it are oblig'd to Duty in their respective Turns. For the Officers Names, Salaries, Allowances, and other Particulars, there is an Account given at the end hereof, but those who desire further information, we refer to Doctor Chamberlayne's present State of England.

This Hospital stands near the same spot of Ground where formerly stood a College, call'd Chelsea College, Erected by King James I for Students in Divinity and History, whose whole Business was to oppose and confute the Errors of the Church of Rome. Doctor Sutcliffe Dean of Exeter was the first Design'd Provost, and Mr. Camden was one of the Members. Notwithstanding the great desire of that Prince, and several Learned Men to see it finish'd, the Building (not to mention the want of Endowment,) could never arrive to farther Perfection than a Shell, and in the time of the late Rebellion, and beginning of King Charles II Reign, it was made use of as a Prison for Dutch Seamen, at last was raz'd to make way for this Magnificent and Beautiful Pile now standing

II. Near the Hospital stands a most Noble seat belonging to the Right Honourable Richard Earl of Ranelaugh, Design'd and Built by himself. His Lordship was one of the first Noble Men in England, that improv'd Gardening to its present Perfection, and his Genius this way is not only lofty, but very happy, as appears by his Gardens, which are Esteem'd the best in England, the bigness consider'd. His House built with Brick, and corner'd with Stone, is not large but very Convenient, and may well be call'd a Cabinet. It stands a good Distance from the Thames near the Middle of his Gardens. In finishing the whole, his Lordship has spar'd neither Labour nor Cost. The very Green houses and Stables (adorn'd with Festoons, Urns, &c.) have an Air of Grandeur, not to be seen in many Princes Pallaces, and which way soever a Man turns his Eyes, he views such Elegancies, as fills him at once with Delight and Wonder. His Lordship generally resides here the greatest part of the Year

III. His Grace the Duke of Beaufort has a Noble Seat at the West end of the Town, which formerly belong'd to Sir George Villars Great Duke of Buckingham. This House is between 2 and 300 Feet in length, has a stately Ancient Front towards the Thames, also Two spacious Court Yards, and behind it are very fine Gardens. 'Tis so pleasantly situated, that the late Queen had a great desire to purchase it before King William built Kensington, but was prevented by some secret obstacles. His Grace the present Duke, is also the Dutchess Dowager, has for some Years past spent their Time at their fine Seat at Badmington in Gloucestershire

IV. The Right Honourable the Countess Dowager of Lindsey has a fair little Home House, next adjoyning to the Duke of Beauforts, said to be built by Sir H. Mayne's Physician to King Charles I It has a very good Front towards the Thames, built after the Modern Manner. The Right Honourable the Countess Dowager of Plymouth, and Lord Windsor her Son resides in it at present.

V. The Right Honourable Anthony Earl of Shaftesbury has built a very neat Seat at little Chelsea, 'tis but small, but admirably well contriv'd, and in time his Gardens now planting will be very fine. His Lordship generally resides here during the sitting of Parliament

VI. The Right Honourable William Lord Cheyne Viscount Newhaven in Scotland, has two very good Seats in this Parish. The one (being the Manhon House) is situated at the East end of the Town near the Thames, and here it was where Queen Elizabeth was Nurst, as said before; the other stands some distance North of the Town, and is call'd Black Land House, both now Let to French Boarding Schools.

VII The Right Reverend Father in God *Peter* Lord Bifhop of *Wintin*, has a Noble Seat here, ftanding next the Lord *Cheyne's* Mannor-houfe, where his Lordfhip has been pleas'd to refide, during the Three laft Seffions of Parliament This Houfe has a good Front and Noble Stair-cafe, with good Rooms and Gardens; 'twas purchas'd and annext to the See of *Winchefter*, by the Learned and Pious Doctor *Andrews* Bifhop of that See, who gave his City Seat at St *Saviours Southwark* to the Poor of that Parifh

VIII At little *Chelfea* ftands a Regular handfome Houfe, with a noble Court Yard, and good Gardens Built by Mr *Marks*, now inhabited by Sir. *John Cope* Baronet, a Gentleman of an Ancient Honourable Family, who formerly was eminent for the Service of his Country Abroad, and for many Years of late, in Parliament, till he voluntary retir'd here to end his Days in Peace.

IX At the Weft end of the Town near the Countefs of *Lindfys*, is a large fpacious Houfe the Building fomewhat Old, formerly the Seat of the Worthy Family of the *Gorges*, in which for many Years paft has been kept a famous Boarding School for young Ladies, by Mr *Jonas Prieft*

X About the Middle of *Church-lane* ftands a very good Houfe, in which dwells Mr *Mofes Goodyear*, a Gentleman well known by moft of the Ingenious Men in the Kingdom, alfo hard by lives Sir *John Munden*, and the Reverend Doctor *John King* Rector

Near the Royal Hofpital, there runs a regular Row of Buildings, towards the *Thames*, call'd *Paradice Row*. In which dwells,

Sir *Thomas Pelham* Baronet, defcended from an Honourable Family. He has been employ'd by the Government in feveral confiderable Pofts, and has for many Years paft ferv'd in Parliament a Knight of the Shire for *Suffex*

Sir *Francis Windham*, Brother to the Honourable Lieutenant General *Windham*, a very Worthy Gentleman of a good Family, who has ferv'd in Parliament feveral Years paft for the *Burrough* of *Ilcefter* in *Sommerfetfhire*.

John Crawford Efq; one of her Majefties Commiffioners,Son to Commiffary *David Crawford*.

Jermyn Wych Efq, one of her Majefties Juftices of the Peace for *Middlefex*, Son to Sir *Cyril Wych* Baronet

Near alfo lives Mr. *Corfellis*, and Mr *John Pennant* both Gentlemen of good Eftates, alfo Mr *John Blow*.

Doctor *Aglionby*, her Majefties Envoy to the *Swifs Cantons* (when in *England*) The Reverend and Learned Doctor *Francis Atterbury* Dean of *Carlile*, and Chaplain in Ordinary to her Majefty, *John Yeats* Efq; Mr *Lucas* Merchant, Mr. *Tobias Humfreys* at little *Chelfea*, Mr *William Turton*, Mr *Marfhall*, Doctor *Frazier* at the College, alfo Mr. *Robert Woodcock*, and Mr. *Charvine* who keeps Boarding Schools for Ladies, and the Reverend Mr *Lefevre*, and Mr *Webfter*, Mafters of Boarding Schools for Young Gentlemen Here are befides feveral other confiderable Perfons, that don't readily occur to our Memory

---

KENSINGTON.

ABout a Mile from *Chelfea* towards the North ftands *Kenfington*, upon a gentle Afcent, a Handfome Populous Place, well fituated on a fine Gravel, and Efteem'd a very good Air What we fhall take notice of here, is

The CHURCH,

Which at prefent is very large and fpacious, built of Brick, and handfomly Finifh'd, but what it was formerly may be guefs'd by the old Tower now ftanding, which has fome appearance of Antiquity, and looks like the Architecture of the Twelfth or Thirteenth Centuries, being but low and built of Flint and rough Stone, with little Art or Order The old Church lately ftanding was of the fame Workmanfhip, and had little in it worth taking notice of, except its Age.

It does not appear this Church was ever dedicated to any Saint, as was ufual, nor can we find after a very ftrict fearch, when or by whom 'twas firft Founded, though we have trac'd its Vicars up to the Year, 1260 When the Abbot of *Abbington* Endow'd it with a Moyety of the great Tythes. What Alterations has fince happen'd we are in the dark about, but find the faid *Abbot* had a Town Houfe near adjoyning to the Church, which ftood where the *Vicars* Houfe now ftands, the remains whereof have been long fince Buried in its own Ruins

Kenfington, being the Place King *William* was pleas'd to fix upon for his Refidence, was during the Courfe of his Reign, fill'd with Perfons of Honour and Diftinction, and grew extreamly in Buildings and Pleafant Retreats. The old Church then much ruin'd and decay'd, was thought not commodious enough for the Reception of fo many Noble Inhabitants, it was therefore

therefore about the Year, 1694 Levell'd with the Ground, except the old Tower, and by the Incouragement and Bounty of several Illustrious Persons fairly Rebuilt, Pav'd, Pew'd, and made very Regular and Convenient, which with all its Furniture Cost about 1800 *l* 300 *l* of which was given by his said Majesty, 100 *l*. by her present Majesty, (then Princess) 50 *l* by the Earl of *Craven*, 50 *l* by the Bishop of *London*, 40 *l*, by the Earl of *Warwick*, and many other considerable Persons gave very liberally toward defraying the Charge of so Pious a Work. The rest was made up by the Subscription of the Inhabitants, and Sale of the Galleries and Pews newly Erected.

The Church thus Rebuilt was in form Quadrangular, somewhat Broader than 'twas long, being near Eighty Feet from North to South, and hardly Seventy from East to West, Pav'd handsomly with Purbeck Stone, the Pewing and Galleries made very Neat and Convenient, and the Pulpit and Chancel handsomely adorn'd with Carving and Painting

But it seems, notwithstanding the great Charge before mention'd, the Work requir'd a greater Expence, or the Managers wanted Judgment or Integrity, for it had not stood Seven Years before the Building was observ'd to Crack, and give way in several Places, and the Walls and Beams were found too Weak for the Weight they were design'd to bear, wherefore in the Year 1704 the Parishioners not thinking themselves safe whilst at their Devotion, agreed to make such Additions and Alterations as was necessary, pursuant to which the whole Roof was taken off, and the North and South Walls pull'd down, almost to the Ground, and Rebuilt again with greater Thickness, and strengthned with Two Butteresses each, the new Beams and Timbers were much stronger, and the whole made firm and substantial, at about 800 *l* Charge to the Inhabitants

Having thus given an Account of the Church in its several Estates, we come to the most considerable part of our Undertaking, *viz.* To view its Monuments Upon Entrance we found nothing that look't like Antiquity, or seem'd Older than the new erected Church, (except a few Grave Stones in the Pavement,) all that was standing before the Demolishing of the old Church, being defac'd and raz'd with it, was buried in its Rubbish 'Tis very reasonable however to believe a Place always so Esteem'd for its Air, might have some considerable Inhabitants inter'd in its Church, but not to make use of Conjectures, when we may be satisfied from undoubted Testimony, Mr *Weaver* assures us there were in it, the following Inscriptions

I *Maud de Berford gift icy,*
Dieu de S'alme est Mercy, Amen

II Here undyr lyeth *Phelip Meawus*, the Son and Heir of *John Meawus*, oone of the Secretaries to the Kings, *Henry* the Seventh and *Henry* the Eighth, Clerk of hys Counsel, and oone of the Knyghts of *Windsor*. *Whyche Philip* decessey the Eight of *November*, MDX, on whoes Soul *Jesu* have Mercy, *Amen*.

III *Hic Jacent* Robertus Rose *&* Eliz. —— Richardus Schardebrugh *&* Elizabetha *Uxor ejus,* ac Robertus Schardebrugh *Filius* —— *eorundem* Richardi *&* Elizabethæ, *qui quidem* Richardus *Obiyt, XI die Decem* M CCCC LIII. *quorum animabus propitietur altissimus*

IV. Here lyes *Adwin Laverock* of *Callis*, Cousin to *John Mautas* of *Kensington*, and French Secretary to King *Hen* the 7th whyche decessevd on Seynt *Stephens* Day, M CCCC L XXXXIII on whose Soul God have Mercy, *Amen*

V. In the Worship of God and our Ladie,
Say for all Christen Souls a Pater Noster, and an Avie.

Hic Jacet Thomas Essex *Armiger Filius & heres* Gulielmus Essex *Armiger, Rememorator Domini Regis* Edwardi —— *quarti in Saccario, ac Vice thesarar Anglica, qui Obiyt* 10th *November,* 1500.

Que sola virgineo nisia, Laudamus honore,
Me protegens, Nato fundito vota tuo

The Monuments in and about it at present are these,

In the CHURCH.

To the Right Hand of the Chancel near the South East Door is fixt in the Wall a plain Monument of black and white Marble, having several Earls Coronets without any Inscription. Over Head is the Ensigns of Honour, belonging to the several noble Persons here Buried, and near the Chancel is the Vault of this Family, made by Sir *Hen. Rich* afterwards Earl of *Holland*, in which are Interr'd.

the said Sir *Hen Rich* Knight of the Garter, afterwards created Baron of *Kensington*, *Ap . . . the Earl of *Holland*, and one of his Majesties Privy Counsel, and Captain of his Guard. He was a younger Brother to the Earl of *Warwick*, Lord high Admiral of *England*

m

in the late Rebellion, and was at laſt for his unſhaken Loyalty to King *Charles* I. together with *James* Duke *Hamilton*, and *Arthur* Lord *Capel* Beheaded. *Anno*, 1649.

II *Robert* Earl of *Holland*, Son of the ſaid Sir *Henry*, who afterward had the additional Title of Earl of *Warwick*, by the Death of *Charles Rich* Earl of that Place his Coz. German. Here Lies alſo *Hen.* and *Cope Rich*, his Brothers.

III *Edward*, Son of *Robert*, by *Anne* Daughter of the Earl of *Mancheſter*, Earl of *Warwick* and *Holland*, alſo ſeveral Ladies, Branches of this Noble Family.

On the left Hand of the Chancel, are plac'd againſt the Wall, Three neat Marble Oval Monuments. That next the Chancel is ſomewhat above Four Foot in length, at the bottom is the Coat encloſ'd with Palm Branches.

Upon the Oval this Inſcription.

M. S.

Henrici Frobock A. M.

viri

Tàm propter mores ſuos quam præcepta
Nunquàm ſatis colendi,
Qui agro Cornubienſi Oriundus,
In celeberrimâ Oxonienſi Academiâ
Omnium diſciplinarum ſtudiis
Exornatus :
In illuſtri Civitate Londinenſi,
quod reliquum erat vitæ ſuæ Tyronibus erudiendis
Fideliter Impendit ;
Poſtquàm utrique Academiæ futuros Alumnos
Enutriendo,
Dotes ab Almâ Matre olim acceptas
piè rependerat.
Ipſe tandem
Ex nimiâ vigilantiâ
Tabe confectus,
Amicis omnibus flebilis Occidit,
Septimo Die Aprilis,
Anno Dom. MDCXCII.
Ætatis Suæ 44.
Hoc Monumentum
Lectiſſima Conjux Margaretta
Mærens P.

In Engliſh thus

Sacred to the Memory
Of *Hen Frobock*, M. A.
A Gentleman
As well for his Manners, as his Precepts,
Never enough to be Eſteem'd
He was Born in the County of *Cornwall*,
And afterwards in the Famous Univerſity of *Oxford*,
With the Studies of Arts and Sciences,
Embelliſh'd
In the flouriſhing City of *London*,
The reſidue of his Life he faithfully imploy'd
In inſtructing Youth
After that to both Univerſities future Scholars
By Educating
The Gifts formerly received from his Alma Mater
He piouſly repaid.
Till at length
By too laborious an Induſtry,
Falling into a Conſumption
By all his Friends he Dies lamented,
The 7th. Day of *April*,
Anno Dom 1691.
In the 44th Year of his Age,
This Monument
His moſt beloved Wife
Lamenting Built.

F

The

The next toward the left Hand in the Middle, is a neat piece of Workmanship near Eight Foot long, Embellifh'd with *Feftoons*, *Foldage* and other Ornaments all of White Marble, behind a loofe Drapery extreamly Natural: The Oval in the middle is a piece of black Polifh'd Marble about Two Foot long, upon which is the following Infcription in Letters of Gold.

NEar this Place lyeth Interr'd the Body of *Thomas Henfhaw* Efq, Born the 15th Day of *June*, 1618 He Married *Anne* the youngeft Daughter, and one of the Coheirs of *Robert Kepping* of *Trwdley*, in the County of *Kent* Efq, by whom He had Six Sons and Two Daughters, Five of his Sons, one Daughter and his Dear and Vertuous Wife, who Died *October* the 10th 1671 lies buried by him

His Daughter *Anne* the only Surviver, is now the Wife of *Thomas Halfey* of great *Hadefdon* in the County of *Hertford* Efq, he had the Honour to be a Gentleman in Ordinary of the Privy Chamber, to King *Charles* and King *James* II by the former he was employ'd fome Years as Envoy Extraordinary to *Chriftian* the 5th King of *Denmark*, and was alfo French Secretary to the latter, and to King *William*, he departed this Life at his Houfe in this Parifh, on the 2d Day of *Jan* MDCLXXXXIX In the 82 Year of his Age

This Monument above, coft near 50*l*

The Third and laft Monument toward the Left Hand, is a plain Oval of black and white Marble, neatly Polifh'd, above Three Foot long, having a Coat at the Top, and upon it this Infcription

HEre beneath this Marble Stone lieth in hopes of a Joyful Refurrection the Body of *Lyonel Ducket* Efq, only Son and Heir of *William Ducket*, late of *Horfhm*, in the County of *Wilts* Efq, by his firft Wife, *Eliz. Henfhaw*. He married *Martha Afh*, Eldeft Daughter of *Samuel Afh* of *Longley* in the County of *Wilts* Efq, by whom he left only Three Sons, *George*, *William*, and *Henry-Stephen* He was Born in this Parifh on the 4th Day of *March*, 1651. and happen'd to depart this Life in this Parifh, on the 5th Day of *December*, MDCXCIII.

Jam mea peracta eft,
Mox veftra agetur, fabula.

My Play is over, and I'm gone,
And prefently your part will Finifh'd be.

Over the preceding Monument even with the North Gallery, is a Monument of black and white Marble with this Infcription.

OVer againft this Place, in the Pew under the Pulpit, there lieth the Body of Mr *Anon Mew* Merchant, who Married *Joannah*, one of the Daughters of *William Mathold* Efq; who departed this Life the 11th. Day of *Jan* in the Year of our Lord, 1658 in the 33d Year of his Age

In the Pavement, at the Foot of the Chancel againft the middle Ifle, lies a large black Stone with this Infcription.

HEre lieth the Body of *Thomas Hodges* D. D. late Dean of *Hereford*, and Vicar of this Parifh, who departed this Life the 22 of *Auguft* A D. 1672 Aged 72 or there abouts
Refurgam

HEre alfo lies the Body of Mrs. *Margaret* the Wife of the above named Dr *Thomas Hodges*, who departed this Life the 14th of *April*, 1696. Aged 75 Years.
Refurgemus.

Upon a white Stone lying near the Doctors.

NEar this Place lieth the Body of *James Worthington* Gentleman, firft Page of the Bed Chamber, to her facred Majefty Queen *Mary*, who after having ferved her full Thirty Years, departed this Life the 19th of *Feb* A. D. 169 in the Forty Seventh Year of his Age

This Stone Covers the Body of Captain *John Worthington* and *Elizabeth* his Wife, (both Servants to her late Majefty,) who was in Command in King *William's* Army, ever fince the Year 168 and in all the Wars in *Ireland* and *Flanders* fince the Revolution, and having feen an Honourable Peace Died the 7th of *Feb* 169 in the 29th Year of his Age

And alfo the Body of *Charlotte Worthington*, only Daughter of *James Worthington* and *Elizabeth* his Wife, who Dyed the 6th. of *March* 169, in the Twenty Second Year of her Age.

Without

Without the CHURCH,

AT the South Eaſt Door ſtands a moſt ſtately and Beautiful Monument of white Marble ; over the Grave is a Tomb about 6 Foot long, 3 Foot broad, and about 3 Foot and an Half High, over that end which joyns to the Church are ſeveral neat Performances in Carving, about Six Foot higher than the Tomb, as an Urn, Feſtoons, &c alſo a Drapery very looſe and natural, ſupported by Two Boys, upon which is the Inſcription The whole, ſecur'd with Iron Spikes about Five Foot high, is the Performance of Mr *Gibbons*, and could not coſt leſs than 130 *l*

Juxtà hic ſub marmoreo tumulo
Jacet Gulielmus Courten, *cuis* Gulielmus *Pater,* Gulielmus *avus,*
Mater Catharina Johannis Comitis de Bridgwater *filia,*
Paternum vel ad Indos præcharum Nomen,
Qui tantis haudquaquam Degener Parentibus,
Summi cum Laude vitæ decurrit tramitem,
Gazarum per Europam Indigator Sedulus,
Quæ is hinc illinc ſibi paritas negavit nemini,
Sed Cupientibus Expoſuit humaniſſimè,
Non Avara mentis pabulum, ſed Ingenii,
Si quid Natura, ſi quid artis Nobile
Opus, id quovis pretio ſuum eſſe Voluit,
Ut Aliys Lucidum conderet ſacrarium :
Aſt Mortis hæc non ſunt Curæ
Hic Muſarum Cultor tam Eximius,
Hic tam inſignis Viator,
Obiit, Quievit 7 *Cal* Apr *A D* 1-02
Vixit Annos 62, *Menſes* 11, *Dies* 28.
Pompam, quam vivus fugit, ne mortuo fieret, teſtamento Cavit,
Sed hoc Qualicumque Monumentum,
Et Quam potuit Immortalitatem
Benè merenti Mærens dedit
Hans Sloane M D.

Engliſh'd thus.

Near this Place under a Marble Tomb
Lies *William Courten,* whoſe Father and Grandfather were *William.*
His Mother *Catharine* was Daughter to *John* Earl of *Bridgwater.*
His Fathers Name was among the *Indians* known,
Who not unworthy of ſo great Progenitors
With higheſt Praiſe run through the Stage of Life,
He was a diligent ſearcher after Treaſures in *Europe,*
Which here and there being gather'd, he deny'd to none,
But with a Bountiful Hand beſtow'd on all that ſought them,
He was not of a covetous, but liberal Temper,
If any Work appear'd curious for Art or Nature,
That he purchas'd and made his own,
Which he devoted to the ſacred Muſes,
Such Gifts as theſe ſurvive Even Death,
——This ſo great Favorite of the Muſes,
And ſo Eminent a Traveller,
Reſted from his Labours the 7th of the *Calends* of *Apr* A D 1-02
He liv'd 62 Years, 11 Months, and Twenty Eight Days
Pomp, which he hated living, by his Laſt Will he forbid to be paid him Dead,
But this Monument (ſuch as it is,)
And ſuch Immortality, as can be given
To a well deſerving Friend, with Grief is offer'd,
By *Hans Sloan* Doctor of Phyſick

There are ſeveral more Tombs and Grave ſtones with Inſcriptions in about this Church, but being ill, of Perſons never taken Notice of in the World, for their Families or Merit, we thought they might without Offence be omitted.

By a certain Inſtrument, bearing Date *Anno* 1260, made between the ſaid Abbot of *Abbington,* and the then Lord Biſhop of *London,* it appears the Right of Collation was then confirm'd to the ſaid Biſhop and his Succeſſors, who now are the perpetual Patrons At the ſame time alſo was annext to the Vicarage, one Moyety of the great Tythe, which he now enjoy'd by the Reverend Doctor *Millington* the preſent Vicar This Vicarage is valued yearly in the Queens Book at 18 *l* 18 *s* 4*d*. but is ſuppos'd worth near, 300 *l per Annum*

The TOWN.

THis Town ſtanding in a wholſome Air, not above Three Miles from *London*, has ever been reſorted to by Perſons of Quality and Citizens, and for many Years paſt Honour'd with ſeveral fine Seats belonging to the Earls of *Nottingham, Warwick*, &c.

We can't indeed find it was ever taken Notice off in Hiſtory, (except for the great Weſtern Road through it, nor hath any thing occur'd in it, that might perpetuate its Name, till his late Majeſty King *William* was pleas'd to Ennoble it with his Court and Royal Preſence. Since which time it has Flouriſh'd even almoſt beyond Belief, and is Inhabited by Gentry and Perſons of Note There is alſo abundance of Shop-keepers, and all ſorts of Artificers in it, which makes it appear rather like part of *London*, than a Country Village.

'Tis with its dependencies, about Three times as big as *Chelſea* in Number of Houſes, and in Summer-time extreamly fill'd with Lodgers for the Pleaſure of the Air, Walks, and Gardens Round it, to the great Advantage of its Inhabitants.

The Buildings are chiefly of Brick, regular and built into Streets, &c the largeſt is that through which the Road lies, reaching from the Queens Houſe a conſiderable way beyond the Church. From the Church runs a Row of Buildings toward the North call'd *Church-lane*, but the moſt Beautiful part of it is the Square, South of the Road, which for Beauty of Buildings and Worthy Inhabitants, exceeds ſeveral noted Squares in *London*

This Pariſh lies toward the North upon *Acton, Wilſdon* and *Paddington*, Eaſt upon St *Margarets Weſtminſter*, and St. *Martins* in the Fields, South upon *Chelſea*, and Weſt upon *Fulham* and *Hammerſmith*, and contains Two Mannours, *viz.* That of Abbot *Kenſington*, and *Earls Court*, beſides ſeveral large Villages, as *Brampton*, part of little *Chelſea, Earls Court*, alſo the *Gravel-pits*, where are ſeveral handſome new built Houſes, and of late Years has been diſcover'd a Famous *Chalybiat* Spring, much eſteem'd and reſorted to for its Medicinal Virtues, but that which adds moſt to the Pleaſures of this Place is *Hide-park* adjoyning, which ſtretcheth it ſelf as far as *Piccadilly*.

Throughout the whole Pariſh is ſcatter'd ſeveral fine Seats, ſome of which (with the Inhabitants) follow

I The Royal Palace at the Eaſt end of the Town, upon the Edge of the Park, formerly the Houſe of the Right Honourable *Heneage* Earl of *Nottingham*, Lord High Chancellor of *England*, &c which King *William* purchas'd with a very large Sum, being the only retreat near *London*, he was pleas'd with. There is but little of the old Houſe now ſtanding, or elſe it appears inconſiderably by the great Additions of new Buildings 'Tis made very neat and convenient, with all the proper Offices, however wants an Air of Grandeur, and looks unlike the Palace of a King The South-eaſt part is a moſt ſtately Pile finely finiſh'd, but this if view'd with the reſt makes the whole ſeem Irregular. But whatever is deficient in the Houſe, is and will be made up in the Gardens, which want not any Advantages of Nature to render them entertaining, and are beautified with all the Elegancies of Art, (Statues and Fountains excepted.) There's a noble Collection of Foreign Plants, and Fine Neat Greens which makes it Pleaſant all the Year, and the Contrivance, Variety, and Diſpoſition of the whole is extream pleaſing, and ſo frugal have they been of the Room they had, that there's not an Inch but what's well improv'd, the whole with the Houſe not being above Twenty Six Acres Her Majeſty has been pleas'd lately to Plant near Thirty Acres more towards the North, ſeparated from the reſt only by a ſtately Green Houſe not yet Finiſh'd, upon this Spot is near 100 Men dayly at Work, and ſo great is the Progreſs they have made, that in leſs than Nine Months the whole is Level'd, laid out and Planted, and when Finiſh'd will be very Fine Mr *Wiſe* her Majeſties Gardener has the Management of this Work

At this Palace their late Majeſties ſpent the greateſt part of their leiſure Hours, and were much pleas'd with its Airy Situation and Pleaſant Proſpects, but valued it moſt for its nearneſs to their Parliament, and 'twas here they both drew their laſt Breath, her Majeſty Dying of the Small Pox, *Decem* 28, 1694 in the 32 Year of her Age, and the King the 8th of *March*, 1702 in his Fifty Second Year, worn out by the Toyls of War, and the Fatigues of an Active Life.

Her Preſent Majeſty with her Royal Conſort, are pleas'd often to ſpend Two or Three Days here in good Weather, and in all probability, deſign to reſide here oftner, when 'tis Finiſh'd This Royal Seat is in the Pariſh of St *Margarets Weſtminſter*.

This Royal Seat, as alſo another at *Wincheſter*, was lately by Act of Parliament ſetled upon his Royal Highneſs the Prince, in caſe he ſhould ſurvive her Majeſty.

II To the Weſt of the Town ſtands a noble Seat call'd *Holland-houſe*, belonging to the Family of the *Rich's* The Situation is very Fine, and the Building ſtately, and full of Antique Ornaments, the Gardens are ſuitable to ſuch a Houſe, and before it is a moſt noble Grove of Elms, above half a Mile in length.

The Counteſs *Dowager*, and *Edward Rich* the preſent Earl of *Warwick*, a Child of great hopes, at preſent reſide here.

III. **Near**

Nearer adjoyning to the Town is another Antient Seat call'd *Compden-house*, formerly the Seat of the Right Noble Viscount *Camden* and Earl of *Gainsborough*

It is a very noble Pile, and finish'd with all the Art the Architects of that time were Masters of. The Situation being upon a Hill makes it extream Healthful and Pleasant. Where the Right Honourable the Countess Dowager of *Burlington*, and *Richard Boyle* the present Earl, Youth of about Twelve Years of Age, of very good Parts Reside.

III. The Honourable Colonel *Guy* has a fine Seat at *Earls Court*. 'Tis but lately Built after the Modern Manner, and standing upon a Plain where nothing can intercept, the Sight looks very thinly at a Distance, his Gardens are very good.

IV. The Honourable the Lady *Bellasis* has likewise a good House here, standing against the Queens Gardens the other side the Road.

V. At *Brompton* the Right Honourable the Marquess of *Mountmont*, General of her Majesties Forces to be employ'd in *Savoy*, *Piedmont*, and Places Adjacent has a Seat.

VI. The Honourable Mr *Seymour* has a fine New built House in the Park, standing upon the Road near *Kensington Gravel-pits*. In *Clinch Lane*, the Square, and near adjoyning dwells likewise Sir *Philip Meadows*, Sir *Hale Hook*, Sir *Humphry Edwin* Aldermen of *London*, Sir *Henry Ashurst*, ———— *Usher* it Esq; one of her Majesties Justices of the Peace for the County of *Middlesex*, the Lady *Wyeman*, the Lady *Beelon*, the Reverend Dr *John Millington*. Also at little *Chelsea* Mr *De Cadinal*, Mr *Palmo*, Mr *Harr*, and Mr *Arnold* at the *Gravel-pits*, where he has a handsome pleasant Seat, with many more Persons of considerable Worth. There is also in Town several noted boarding Schools, but mostly for Young Gentlemen. And in this Parish is that Spot of Ground call'd *Brompton-Park*, so much Fam'd all over the Kingdom, for a Nursery of Plants, and fine Greens of all sorts, which supply most of the Nobility and Gentlemen in *England*. This Nursery was rais'd by Mr. *London* and Mr *Wise*, and now tis Brought to its greatest Perfection, and kept in extraordinary Order, in which a great number of Men are constantly Employ'd. The stock seems almost Incredible, for if we believe some who affirm that the several Plants in it were valued at but 1 *d* a piece, they would amount to above 40000 *l*

THE following Account from the Reverend Mr *Charles Seward*, not coming to our Hands before the Press was set, and the Sheets of *Kensington* Work'd off, we could not insert it in its proper Place, however it being very particular, and containing a curious Account of the Seats and Mannors in that Parish, we thought it might not be improper to add it here in the Authors own Words.

I Think it proper in the first Place to Mention, what has come to my Knowledg relating to the Estate in the Mannor of *Abbots Kensington*, now belonging to the Earl of *Warwick, &c.* before I proceed to answer your Questions. In the Reign of King *Henry* I it appertain'd to the Family of the *Vere's*, and how 'twas then dispos'd of, you may read in the following Transcript, Ex Regist. in Biblioth Cottoman f 137 De Ecclesia de Kinsintune *Godfridus de Vere Albrici senioris filius, Albrici minoris frater, suorum fratrum in nascentia primus, ac ideo in hæreditate paterna successor futurus, tum morum, quam parentum generositate admodum inclitus, Abbatem medinus se gratia ad Fbricium contulit, Erat enim gravi correptus morbo, Tribus ergo ab Abbate et curá mensibus impensá, id quá pulsab itur, convalu t molestiá. Sed quia contra mortem nulla est medicina, alius morbus hunc occup it cogens ed cedere vitá. Itaq, instante temporis ipsius articulo idem æger Ecclesiam sui patrimonii de Villá Kinsintuná patre suo Albrico & matre suá Beatrice, una cum fratribus suis idem concedentibus perpetuá donatione Abbendinensi Monasterio contulit, cum duarum hidarum, duodecies viginti acris terræ disterminatá, et insuper unius Virgitæ portione, cujus doni Auctoritatem Regis quoq, hujusmodi confirmavit Edictum*

Carta R Hen I de Ecclesia de Kinsintune   *Inter Ann* 1100 & 1107

Hen Rex Anglor Mauritio Londinensi Episcopo, Gilberto Abbati Westmonasterii & Hugoni de Bochelonda, & omnibus Baronibus suis & Ministris Francis & Anglis de Lundonia & Middlesexia Salutem Sciatis me concessisse in tempore Fbricii Abbatis Ecclesiæ Sanctæ Mariæ in Abbendonia, Ecclesiam de Chensnetuna & quicquid ad eam pertinet Et terram in ipsa Villa inter Ecclesiam & terram aliam duarum hidarum de duodecies viginti acris quam Albricus de Vere dedit prædict. Ecclesiæ pro anima Goffredi filii sui defuncti, ut eam Ecclesiam in pace in perpetuum & quiete teneat Testibus Matilda Regina, Eudone Dapifero, & Willielmo de Curceio, & Nigello & Csitio, Ursone de Albriot, Roberto malet apud Corneberiam.

> *Cedunt è vitâ votis animisque cupitâ*
> *Barbarus & scita Gentilis & Israelita,*
> *Has pariter metas habet omnis sexus, & ætas,*
> *En puer, en senior, pater alter, filius alter*
> *Egrem, fortunam, terram venere sub unam*
> *Non juvenis totæ quas epotavit Athenæ,*
> *Non vetulo notæ vires vel opes valuere,*
> *Sed valuere fides & prædia quæ memoramus,*
> *Ut valeant valeant per secula cuncta precamur*

G

In

In the 44th Year of King *Hen* III *An. Dom* MCCLX, and 281 Years before the diffolving of the Monafteries and Abbies in the 31 Year of King *Hen* VIII *An Dom* MDXI, by a Compofition, between the then Abbot of *Abindon*, and the Vicar of *Kenfington*, it was agreed, that the Vicar, and his Succeffors fhould have a Moyety of the greater Tythes, an that the Collation of the Vicarage fhall remain to the Bifhop of *London*, and to his Succeffors the Bifhops for ever *pleno Jure*, and it appears in the feveral Books of Records in his Regifters Office, that all the Vicars from the Year MCCCXXII, [the Records before that time being deftroy'd by the dreadful Fire in *London*, *An* MDCLXVI] to the Year MDCC, incluſively, have been collated by the Bifhops of *London*

From the 31 of King *Hen* VIII, *An Dom* MDXI, to the 11 of Queen *Eliz* MDLIX, the Mannor and Parſonage [belonging to the Abby of *Abindon*] in the Parifh of *Kenfington*, were in the Crown, and then purchas'd of her Majefty by *Walter Cope* Gent who [the Year following fold the Manfion Houfe, call'd the Mannor or Parfonage Houfe, with the Lands and Tythes thereunto appertaining, to *Robert Hofman* Gent

The Two Seats now call'd *Holland* and *Campden* Houfe were Built, and alfo [if I am not mifinform'd] that lately the Earl of *Nottingham*, fituate in the Parifh of St *Margaret* in *Weft-minfter*, by Mr *Cope* but in what Year I cannot certainly tell, the Two firft, if not the laft, were erected, as I have often heard, before the Death of Queen *Elizabeth*

The firft of thofe Seats with the Mannor of *Abbots Kenfington* [as alfo the Mannor of *Earls Court*, in the faid Parifh, bought by Sir *Walter Cope*, of a Knight whofe Name I cannot call to Mind] Sir *Henry Rich* Knight of the *Bath*, [and fecond Son to *Robert* the firft Earl of *Warwick* of this Family] became poffefs'd of, by mairying *Ifabella* the Daughter and Heir to the faid Sir *Walter Cope*, by whom he had Four Sons, *Robert*, *Charles*, *Henry*, and *Cope*, and Five Daughters By Letters Patent, bearing date *March* the 8th 1622 *An R Jacobi* 20, he was advanc'd to the Dignity of a Baron of this Kingdom, by the Title of Lord *Kenfington*, and upon the 24th of *September*, 1621 *An R Jac* 20, he was created Earl of *Holland* [a Province in *Lincolnfhire*] and fhortly after was inftall'd Knight of the moft noble Order of the Garter To him fucceeded in his Honors and Eftate, *Robert* his eldeft Son, whofe firft Wife was---- Daughter to Sir *Arthur Ingram* of *Temple Newfom* in the County of *York*, by whom he had Iffue divers Children, which Died in his Life time His Second Wife was *Anne*, the Daughter of *Edward* Earl of *Manchefter*, by whom he had Iffue *Edward*, and Three Daughters *Charles* Earl of *Warwick*, Dying *Auguft* 24th 1673, without Iffue, the Dignity of Earl of *Warwick*, and thofe other Titles which he enjoy'd, thereupon devolv'd to this *Robert* Earl of *Holland*, his neareft Kinfman of the Male-line, but no more of his Eftate, than *Warwick-houfe* in *Holbourn*. *Robert* Earl of *Warwick* and *Holland* departing this Life in *April* 1675, to him fucceeded *Edward* his Son and Heir, who married *Charlotte* the Daughter of Sir *Thomas Middleton* of *Chirk-caftle* in the County of *Denbigh* Baronet, and Grand-daughter of Sir *Orlando Bridgman* Baronet, Lord Keeper of the Great Seal of *England*, from *September* the 4th 1667, to *November*, 1672, and by her had Iffue *Edward-Henry*, the prefent Earl of *Warwick* and *Holland*, his Father Dying----

The Second Seat call'd *Campden-houfe*, was purchas'd, or won [as it hath been commonly reported many Years fince by fome of the Antient Parifhioners] at fome fort of Game of Sir *Walter Cope* by Sir *Baptift Hicks*, afterwards created Lord *Hicks* of *Ilmington* in *Warwickfhire*, and Vicount *Campden* of *Campden* in *Gloucefterfhire*, 5 *Maii* 4 *Caroli An Do* 1629, with remainder [for default of Iffue-Male of his Body] to *Edward* Lord *Noel* Baron of *Ridlington* in the County of *Rutland* [advanc'd to that Degree and Dignity, 23 *Martii*, 14 *Jacobi* 1616] and to the Heirs-Male in his Body, who married *Julian*, the Daughter and Cohen of Sir *Baptift Hicks* Knight, upon his advancement to the Titles of Baron of *Ilmington*, and Vicount *Campden*, and had Iffue by her Two Sons, *Baptift* and *Henry*, and Two Daughters, *Elizabeth* married to Sir *Erafmus de la Fountain* of *Kirby-Bellers* in the County of *Leicefter*, Knight, and *Penelope* to *John* Vicount *Chaworth*, and departing this Life in the Kings Garrifon at *Oxford*, 10 *Martii*, 19 *R Caroli*, 1643, *Baptift* his Son and Heir fucceeded him, who by his Third Wife *Hefter*, one of the Four Daughters and Coheirs of *Thomas* Lord *Wotton*, Baron of *Marley* in *Kent*, had Iffue Two Sons, *Edward* and *Henry*, and Four Daughters, and by his Fourth Wife *Elizabeth*, Daughter of *Mountague*, late Earl of *Lindfey* [upon whom was fettled, and the Heirs Male of her Body *Campden-houfe* as part of her Jointure] he had Iffue Three Sons, *Lindfey*, who Died an Infant, *Baptift*, and *John*, and Three Daughters *Edward* his Eldeft Son fucceeded him, and married *Elizabeth* the Daughter of *Thomas* late Earl of *Southampton*, and by her had Iffue one Son, *Wriothfley Baptift* [who Died before him] and Three Daughters, the Second of *December*, *An R Caroli* II 1682, he was made Earl of *Gainsborough* *Elizabeth* Vicountefs Dowager *Campden* Dying *An* 1634, *Baptift* her Eldeft Son became Poffeffor of *Campden houfe* he married ----- the Daughter of Sir *Thomas Fanfhaw* of *Jenkins* in the Parifh *Barking*, and County of *Effex* Knight, and had Iffue by her a Son named *Baptift*, and one Daughter, but Dying in *July* 1691, and before *Edward* Earl of *Gainsborough* his half Brother [who departed this Life- ------, *Baptift* the Son of the faid *Baptift* fucceeded him in his Honours and Eftate, and is at this time Earl of *Gainsborough*

A

A LIST of the Salaries of Officers and Servants belonging to the Royal Hospital at *Chelsea.*

	£	s.
THE Governour	500 *l.*	0
Lieutenant Governour	200	0
Major	150	0
First Chaplain .	100	0
Second Chaplain	100	0
Physician	100	0
Secretary and Clerk	100	0
Deputy Treasurer	100	0
Comptroller	50	0
Steward	50	0
Surgeon	73	0
Apothecary	50	0
Surgeons Mate	20	0
Clerk of the Works	20	0
Wardrobe-keeper	40	0
Master Cook	40	0
Second Cook	30	0
Master Butler and Servants	35	0
Three Under Cooks	30	0
Scullery, Man and Servants	40	0
Sexton	16	0
Usher of the Halls	20	0
. Porter	12	0
Two Sweepers	20	0
House-keeper	90	0
Twenty four Matrons	192	0
Barber	60	0
Canal keeper and Turn lock	20	0
Yeoman of the Coal yard	20	0
Gardener and Servants	260	0
Water-Engine-keeper	20	0
Lanthorn keeper	20	0
Organist and Repairs	26	0
Bucket-mender	8	0
Clock maker, for cleaning the Clock	6	0
Adjutant	20	0
A supernumerary Matron	3	0
The Tythe free Ground *per Ann.* to { *Chelsea*	18	9
{ *Kensington*	02	0
Total of Salaries, &c. *per Ann.*	2621	9

From these large Salaries a just estimate may be made of the handsom Allowances and Provision made for all the Members belonging to this House, which in this particular as well as in Building, &c. exceeds all the Charitable Foundations in *Europe.*

Benefactors to the Poor of the Parish of *Chelsea*.

THE Honorable *Charles* Lord *Cheyne*
The Lady *Jane Cheyne* his Wife
The Honorable Mr *Ashburnham*
Sir *Joseph Alstone* Barronet
Baldwyn Amy Doctor of Physick
Mr *Ralph Palmer* his Nephew

{ All great Benefactors, especially towards Repairing the Church, Building the Steeple furnishing it with Bells, and a Clock, &c

The Right Honorable the Lady *Anne Dacres*, by Will, dated *Anno* 1595, hath provided that certain Poor Men and Women of the Parish of *Chelsea*, shall be sent to her Hospital at *Westminster* and taken care of during Life, and that when any happens to dye their Places to be fill'd up by others from this Parish

To the POOR

The Lady *Stenehorse* gave by Will in 1645 *per Ann* to buy Bread the summ of   20 *l.*

Mr *Charles Plucknet* gave by Will in 1654 *per Ann* to buy Bread the summ of   20 *l.*

Mr *James Ashton* gave by Will in 1657 the summ of Forty Pounds, to be lent to Eight poor Tradesmen in *Chelsea* for Two Years, that is, Five Pounds to each, which when call'd in, is to be lent by the Church-wardens to Eight other poor Traders.   40 *l*

Mr *James Larrett* gave by Will in 1662 the summ of Ten Pounds *per Ann* for ever, to be distribute quarterly by the Church-wardens, &c   10 *l.*

Mr *Richard Gilford* gave by Will in 1680 the summ of Ten Pounds *per Ann* for ever, Eight Pounds whereof is to be equally distributed to Sixteen poor Men and Women, one Guinea for a Sermon to the Minister of the Parish, the rest to the Clerk and for the Ringers Dinner   10 *l.*

Edward Chamberlayne L L D in consideration of a Vault for his Family in the Church-yard, gave Five Pounds *per Ann.* for ever, to find a poor Boy of *Chelsea* to a Waterman of *Chelsea*, as is mentioned upon his Monument.   5 *l.*

Benefactors to the Poor of the Parish of *Kensington*.

UPon the back side of the *Kings Arms* in the Church of *Kensington*, is an account of Benefactions to the Parish, but the Letters being decayed and in some places quite worn out, we could not be so particular as we could wish, nor discover in many places the dates. The most confiderable Benefactions towards the re-building and repairing the Church we have already taken notice of

The Right Honorable Sir *Bapt Hicks* Vicount *Campden* gave in Lands for ever *per Ann.*   14 *l.*
The Right Honorable Viccountels *Campden* gave to the Poor for ever *per Ann.*   12 *l*
Mr *Tho Goodfellow* gave by Will *per Ann* about the Year 1596   1 *l*
John Powel Gent gave *per Ann* about the Year 1604   1 *l.*
The Lady *Bartlet* gave *per Ann* about the Year 1617   10 *l.*
Tho Young Yeoman of the Guard to Q *Elizabeth* give *per Ann*   1 *l.*
Mr. *Pimble* gave to the Poor for ever *per Ann*   8 *l.*
Mr. *Sams* gave to the Poor for ever *per Ann*   5 *l.*
Oliver (we suppose *Cromwell*) gave to the Poor for ever *per Ann*   3 *l.*

In all *per Ann.*   55 *l*

There is an Account of other Benefactions, as Church Plate and Ornaments, which is very difficult to be discover'd The following Account was transmitted by a Gentleman who has been an Antient Inhabitant in that Parish

All the Benefactions now mention'd are punctually paid according to the Directions of the Pious and Charitable Persons above-named

The End of the First Part.

The Second PART,

OF THE

ANTIQUITIES

OF

MIDDLESEX;

Being a COLLECTION of the feveral

Monuments and Inscriptions,

In the Parish CHURCHES of

Fulham, Hammerfmith, Chifwick and *Acton.*

Alfo an Hiftorical ACCOUNT of each

CHURCH and PARISH;

WITH

The Seats, Villages, and Names of the moft Eminent Inhabitants, &c.

Preparing for the Prefs, PART III. which will contain, the Parifhes of *Ealing, New Brentford, Thifhleworth,* and *Hanwell.*

LONDON,

Printed by *W. Redmayne, for S. Keble* at the Great *Turk's-Head* in *Fleetfreet, D. Brown* at the *Black Swan* and *Bible* without *Temple-bar, A Roper* at the *Black Boy* in *Fleetfreet, R. Smith* at the *Angel* and *Bible* without *Temple-bar,* and *F. Coggan* in the *Inner-Temple-Lane,* MDCCVI.

TO THE

Right Reverend Father in God,

HENRY,

Lord Bifhop of *London*, Dean of the Chappel Royal,
and One of the Lords of Her Majefties Moft
Honourable Privy Council, *&c.*

AND TO

The Honourable

Sir STEPHEN. FOX, Kt.

This Collection,

Of the Antiquities and Funeral Monuments, in the
Parifhes of *Fulham*, *Hammerfmith*, *Chifwick*, and *Acton*,
in the County of *Middlefex*.

I S

Moft humbly Dedicated and Devoted,

B Y

His Lordfhips, and his Honours,

Moft Humble,

Moft Obedient,

and Moft Devoted Servant,

John Bowack.

THE
ANTIQUITIES
OF
MIDDLESEX, &c.

PART. II

FULHAM

Proceeding with the Courfe of the River *Thames* towards the Weft, according to our propos'd Method, the next Parifh we meet with upon its Northern Banks, is *Fulham*, which according to Learned *Camden* (*Britannia p* 310 laft *E*) in Saxon *Fullon-ham* that is, a Houfe of Fowls · In all Probability a Place where all forts of Land and Water Fowls were Bred and Preferv'd for the Diverfion of our Saxon Monarchs, being very well fitted by Nature for fuch a Ufe, and formerly well fhaded with Trees and Pleafant Groves, and very well water'd, efpecially the South Parts of it, which lies Low, and is frequently wafh'd by the gentle Rifings and Excurfions of the *Thames*, which almoft environs the whole Parifh This agrees with Mr *Norden's* Conjectures about its Name, Commenting upon the aforefaid Paffage of *Camden* ' *Fulham* (fays he) of the Saxons called *Fullonham* which (as ' Mafter *Camden* taketh it) fignifieth *Volucrum Domus*, the Habitacle of Birds or the Place of ' Fowles, *Fullon* and *Fuglas* in the Saxon Toong Signifie Fowles and *Ham* or *Hame* as much as ' Home in our Toong So that *Fullon Ham* or *Fuglafhame* is as much as to fay the Home Houfe ' or Habitacle of Fowle *Ham* alfo in many Places fignifieth *Amnis* a River But it is moft pro- ' bable it fhould be of Land Fowle which ufually Haunt Groves and Clufters of Trees, where- ' of in this Place it feemeth hath been Plenty. The Dimenfions of this Parifh is large, extending it felf from a fmall Creek at Sand End near *Chelfea* in the Eaft to the Brick Kiln near *Chifwick* in the Weft (including the Bounds of it's Chappel of Eafe of *Hammerfmith*) in all by the *Thames* Side about Three Miles, it Shoots it felf in a narrow Slip North Weft as far as *Wildon* about Five Miles, and Ends almoft in a Point It bounds North and North Faft upon *Afton* and *Kenfington*, Eaft as before upon *Chelfea*, South Eaft, South, and South Weft upon the River *Thames*, which forms the Shore almoft into a Semicircle by it's Pleafant winding, and takes in Part of that Ifland of *Ofiers* in it near *Chifwick* call'd *Mickenfhaw* Fight, and Weft and Northweft upon *Wildon*, *Ealing* and *Afton*. This Place Boafts of fome things Remarkable, and is beautified with feveral Fine Seats and Large Villages, which fhall be Confider'd af- ter we have Survey'd the Church and its Monuments

THE CHURCH

This Church ftanding a fmall Diftance from the Water Side is Built of Stone, and does not feem to be of any Great Antiquity, the Tower at the Weft End being in a very good Condition is well as the Body of the Church It has not been Patch'd up fince it's firft Erection, fo is to make any confiderable Alteration in the whole Building, not has there been any Additions made is is ufual in Ancient Structures, (except of a fmall Building for a School, &c at the North Door) but, both Tower and Church feem of the fame Age and manner of Workmanfhip We were in hopes whatever Imperfect Accounts have been left of the Foundation of other Churches, yet that here we fhould not have wanted Light, fince 'tis fituated fo near the Tillop of *London* Seat, which appears to be much Ancienter, but after the moft Inquifitive fearch, we could Difcover nothing at all, nor fo much as either to whom 'tis Dedicated However from a very careful Examination of the Building, we conclude it was Built about the beginning of the Fifteenth Century At the North Entrance againft the Wall are feveral Coats of Arm on each fide the Door [probably of the Founders] fome of which are quite Defac'd, and the others fo worn and fullied that there hardly remains any thing from which Light may be gather'd Had thefe been carefully preferved or for-

H early

merly taken Notice of by any that Writ on this Subject by knowing the Founders, we might have known the Time of its Founding, but all have silently pafs'd them over, nor can any of the moft Ancient Inhabitants give any Account of an Infcription quite Defac'd now, under one of the Coats of Arms.

As to the Alterations and Repairs that have been made in this Church, they feem to have been but very few, as before. We find in the Regifter Book of this Parifh, that Dr *Edwards* the Bifhop of *Londons* Chancellor, a great Benefactor to this Church gave by Will, dated *Jan* 9th. 1618, Fourfcore Pounds towards its Repair, which was laid out in making a Gallery, in New Cafting the Lead of the Steeple, and Cieling the Church, he likewife gave Sixteen Pounds long before his Death for Building a New Veftry, School-houfe, and Lodgings for the Mafter, Clark and Sexton, which with other Monies rais'd in the Parifh for that Purpofe were apply'd to the faid ufe, which Building was Erected at the North Door joyning to the Church about the Year 1630 There happened no other general Repair till the Year 1686, when by the Induftry of Mr. *Robert Limpany* then Church Warden, the Church was New Roof'd, Beautified, Enlightned, and the Infide made more Commodious at about One Hundred and Sixty Pounds Charge to the Parifh.

The Monuments and Infcriptions.

This Church has been the Repofitory of the Afhes of many Confiderable Perfons, and there are fome Monuments now ftanding that appear very ftately, (the Infcriptions of which Time has depriv'd us of) which evince this There are now ftanding in it likewife, feveral Beautiful and Noble Monuments lately Erected, but before we take notice of them, we fhall Tranfcribe fome Infcriptions from Mr. *Weaver*, which he fays formerly were in this Church, though there is but one now left Legible, feveral Stones having had their Brafs Plates with the Effigies, *&c.* Torn off in that wretched Havock made in the late horrid Rebellion.

Mr *Weaver* begins with the Monument of Sir *Ralph Butts* [Funeral Monuments p 525.] (as he calls him by Miftake, his Name being *William*) now ftanding with the Infcription in Englifh, (feveral Words being Spelt according to the Cuftom of that Time, as if it had been exactly tranfcrib'd,) though we found it in Latin as follows.

On a plain Stone againft the Wall in the Chancel.

Epitaphium Gulielmi Buttis Equitis Aurati & Medici Regis
Henrici Octavi, Qui Obiit Anno Domini, MDXLV, 17. *Novembris.*

Quid Medicina valet ; quid honos : quid gratia Regum ;
  Quid popularis Amor, mors ubi fæva venit ?
Sola valet PIETAS, quæ ftructa eft, aufpice Chrifto,
  Sola in Morte valet, cætera cuncta fluunt.
Ergo mihi in vita fuerit, quando omnia, Chriftus,
  Mori mihi nunc lucrum, vitaque, Chriftus erit.

Then follow (which Mr *Weaver* has omitted) Thefe Words

Epitaphium hoc primitus Infcriptum pariete, & fitu jam penè
Erafum, fic demum, reftituit Leonardus Butts Armiger
Norfolciensis October 30, 1627.
                Amoris G.

Underneath is his Tomb rais'd above Two Foot from the Ground, upon which in Brafs is reprefented an armed Knight, (the Infcription being taken away) and at his left Hand a Deaths Head with thefe Words *Myn Advantage* At each Corner of the Stone his Arms

The Infcription above in Englifh.

1. The Epitaph of Sir *William Butts* Knight Phyfician to King *Henry* the VIII who Died *Anno Domini* 1545, the 17th. of *November.*

What avails Skill, Honour, or Royal Favour ?
Or Publick Fame, when Death relentlefs comes ;
Piety's only the true lafting good,
Our fole Comfort in Death, when all things elfe forfake us,
Since then Chrift while I Liv'd to me was all,
Death now is gain, for Chrift will be my Life.

This Epitaph firft infcribed on the Wall, and almoft worn out and defac'd, was thus at length Reftor'd, by *Leonard Butts* of *Norfolk* Efq, the 30th. of *October*, 1627.
                                        Mr.

Mr. *Weaver* besides has these following, *Ibid.* 526. Pray for the Sowls of *John Long* Gentylman, *Katherine* and *Alice* his Wyfs. Who Dyed the X of *March* one Thowsand Fyve Hundryd and Three, on whos Sowls and all Christen Sowls Jesu have Mercy.

Fili redemptor mundi Deus miserere nobis
Sancta Trinitas unus Deus miserere nobis
Spiritus Sanctus Deus miserere nobis.

Hic jacet Johannes Sherburne Bachalaureus utriusque Legis, quondam Archidiaconus Essex. qui obijt 1434

Of your Cherite Pray for the Soul of Sir *Sampson Norton* Knight, late Master of the Ordinance of Warre with Kyng *Henry* the Eyght, and for the Soul of Dame *Elysabyth* his Wyff Which Syr *Sampson* Deceisyd the Eyght Day of *February* one Thousand Fyve Hundry'd and Seventeene.

Orate pro anima Johannis Thorley Armigeri, qui obijt penultimo die men: Feb. Ann. Dom. 1645
Hic jacet Magister Willelmus Harvy *nuper vicarius istius Ecclesie qui obijt 5 Die Novemb.* 1471
Hic jacet Georgius Chauncy quondam Receptor Generalis Reverendi Patris Domini Ric. Fitz-James London Episcopi. qui obiit decimo None Die Decembris Ann Dom 1520
Hic jacet Domicilla Margareta suandin nat. Gandius Frandris, que ex Migistro Gerardo hornebolt Gaudauensi pretoris nominatissimo peperit Domicillam Susannam Uxorem Johannis Parker Arcuarii Regis. que obiit Anno Domini, 1529. 26 *Novembris*
Hic jacet Anna Sturton filia Johannis Sturton Domini de Sturton & Domine Katherine Uxoris ejus. Que quidem Anna Obiit in Assumptionem beate Marie Virginis Anno Dom 1533.
Hic jacet Lora filia Johannis Blount Militis Domini Mountjoy & Lore Uxoris ejus. que obiit 6 die Men · Febr. Anno Domini 1480. *Cujus Anime Deus sit propitius.*

Stow likewise Mentions these following in this Church

Hic situs est Gulielmus Billesby Equet Auratus, Fisci Regis ostiarius, cum Anna Uxore, è Familia Brograuia que illi peperit duas Filias, Franciscam, & Margaretam totidemque Filias, qui infantes obierunt.
Obiit ille 25 *Martii* 1607.
Illa 27 *Maii* 1608.

Francisca Filia primogenita, primum nupta Joanni Madocks Armigero, postea Thomæ Walker Armigero Fisci Regis ostiario Obiit die 6 Novembris 1607. *& hic parentibus tumulatur Margar. altera Filia enupta Hugoni Parlor de Plumsted Armigero Obiit & in Ecclesia Sanct. Margaretæ Westmonasterii* Requiescit.

At Earth in Corwal was my first beginning,
From Bonds and Carringtons as it may appear
Now to Earth in *Fulham* God dispoeeth my Ending
In *March* the Thousand and Six Hundred Year,
Of Christ, in whom my Body here doth Rest
Till both in Body and Soul I shall be fully Blest.
Thomas Bond Obiit Anno Ætatis suæ, 68.

Now standing in this Church

In the Chancel
On the right Hand against the Wall A plain Monument Rais'd about 10 Foot from the Ground having over Head the Arms of Sir *Thomas Smith* and his Lady

Under on a Polish'd Stone this Inscription

D. O. M.
THOMÆ SMITHO Equiti Aurato Regiæ Majestatis
Supplicum libellis & ab Epistolis Latinis
Vero Doctrina Prudentiaque singulari
Francisca Gul. Baronis Chandos Filia
Opt. Marito Conjux Mœstissi.
Plorans posuit
Obiit xxviii die Nov. MDCIX.

In

, . . , . In English thus. .

To *Thomas Smith* Knight Master of Requests and Latin Secretary to the Kings Majesty, a Man of singular Learning and Prudence, Frances Daughter of *William* Lord Chandois, his Melancholy Wife as a Proof of her affection to the best of Husbands, Erected and Dedicated this Monument.
He Died the 28th. of *November*, 1609.

On the left Hand.

A very Ancient Monument against the Wall Beautified with Oak Leaves, Flowers and other Antique Ornaments, and within a large Nitch in Brass Plates, the Effigies of a Man and Woman Kneeling with an Inscription which is defac'd, also Two Plates having Inscriptions not legible now.

A Neat Ancient Monument Rais'd about Twelve Foot from the Ground, and secur'd with Iron Rails, in which between Two Corinthian Pillars is the Effigies of the beautiful Lady Lech near as big as the Life, with an Infant in swadling Cloaths in her Arms, and another lying by her, all very well done for that time Over head is the Coat of the Family neatly done

And below on the Tomb as follows.

TO THE MEMORY

Or what else Dearer remayneth of that Vertuous Lady I a *Margaret Lech* Daughter of him, that sometimes was Sir *Gilbert Gerrard* Kt and Master of the Rolles in the Highe Courte of Chancery, Wiffe to Sr. *Peter Lech* of Lyme in the County of *Chester* Knight, and by him the Mother of Seven Sons *Pierce, Frauncis, Radcliffe, Thomas, Peter, Gilbert* and *John* ; with Two Daughters *Anne* and *Katherine* ; of which *Radcliffe, Gilbert, John* Deceased Infants, the rest yet surviving to the happy Increase of their House. The Years she enjoyed the World were XXXIII, her Husband Enjoy'd her XVII, at which period she yielded her Soul to the blessedness of long Rest and her Body to this Earth, *July* 3d. MDCIII

This Inscription in the Note of Piety and Love
by her sad Husband is here
Devotedly placed

In the Chancel Pavement

On a large Stone (the Inscription being gone) the Effigies of an Armed Man, and at each Corner of the Stone his Coat of Arms Probably this may be the Grave Stone of Sr *William Billesby* before mention'd taken Notice of by *Stow*.

A large Black Stone upon which is the following Inscription

Here lyeth interred the Body of Captain *John Saris* of *Fulham* in the County of Middlesex Esquire, he departed this Life the Eleventh Day of *December* 1643 Aged 63 Years He had to Wife *Anne* the Daughter of *William Migges* of *London* Esquire, she departed this Life the Second Day of Feb *Anno Dom* 1622 and lyes Buried in the Parish Church of St *Buttolph* in *Thames Street* being Aged 21 Years.

On another Stone adjoyning of the same Size, a Coat neatly done and this Inscription.

Here lyeth the Body of *William Rumbold* Esq, Clarke and Comptroler of his Majesties great Wardrobe, and Surveyer General of all the Customs of *England*, who Dy'd the Second of *May*, 1667, and also the Body of *Mary* his Wife only Daughter of *Berkly* Esq, of the Body to his late Majesty K. *Charles* the first of blessed Memory. She Dyed the 21 of *August* following

At the Foot of the Chancel Steps upon Old Stone without any Inscription is the Effigies of a Clergyman, &c in his Habit

In this Chancel as also in many Places of the Body of the Church are several Escutcheons and other Ensigns of Honour belonging to such Noble Persons here interr'd in Vaults, which have no other Monuments

In

This Monument following *Stow* places in *Chelsea* Church by miſtake
In the South Iſle or South Chancel
On the Right Hand againſt the Wall a Neat Monument of Alabaſter with black and red
Marble, adorn'd after the Ancient Manner, with this Inſcription

SACRÆ MEMORIÆ GULIELMI PLUMBE ARMIGERI
ET ELIZABETHÆ UXORIS EJUSDEM

Gulielmus Plumbe Filius & hæres Johannis Plumbe de Eltham Armi-
geri, duas Uxores duxit, priorem Margaretam, filiam & Unicam hæ-
redem Thomæ Nevil Equitis, quam Robertus Southwell Eques, vi-
duam Reliquerat, ex qua nullam prolem genuit, alteram Elizabeth'm,
ex qua unicus ei filius natus eſt Franciſcus Plumbe, Elizabetha
unica filia & hæres Edvardi Dormer de Fulham Armigeri filii natu
minimi Galfridi Dormer de Thame Armigeri. Priorem Conjugem
habuit Johannem Greſham de Mayfield in Com Suſſexiæ Armigerum
& Secundum Filium Johannis Greſham Equitis (Quondam Maj-
London) cui tres peperit Filios, Thomam Gulielmum & Edvardum
Greſham. eo Defuncto, Gulielmum Plumbe Prædictum, conjugem
accepit Gulielmus Plumbe Obiit 9 Die Februarii Anno Domini
MDLXXXXIII Annique Ætatis ſuæ LX Elizabetha Plumbe Obiit
Annoque Domini. Annoque Ætatis ſuæ

In Engliſh thus
SACRED TO THE MEMORY OF *WILLIAM PLUMBE* ESQUIRE
AND *ELIZABETH* HIS WIFE.

William Plumbe Son and Heir of *John Plumbe* of Eltham Eſq,
Married Two Wives, the firſt *Margaret* Daughter and Sole
Heireſs of *Thomas Nevil* Gent. (whom Sr *Robert Southwell* At
left a Widow by whom he had no Iſſue, the other *Elizabeth* by
whom he had one only Son *Francis Plumbe* *Elizabeth* was Sole
Daughter and Heireſs of *Edward Dormer* of *Fulham* Eſq,
Youngeſt Son of *Galfrid Dormer* of *Thame* Eſq, She had for
her firſt Husband *John Greſham* of *Mayfield* in the County of
Suſſex Eſq, and Second Son of Sir *John Greſham* (formerly Lord
Major of *London*) to whom She bore Three Sons, *Thomas*, *William*,
and *Edward Greſham*.

After his Death ſhe Married the aboveſaid *William Plumbe*,
He Died the 9th of *October*, 1593 And in the 60th Year of his Age
Elizabeth Plumbe Died in the Year of our Lord   and in
the   Year of her Age

This Monument as appears was Erected in the Life time of Mr *Plumbe* by the ſpaces left
for the time of her Age and Death, and whether ſhe was Buried here or no, is uncertain
tho that ſhe was not, ſeems moſt probable

A very Beautiful tho' Plain Modern Monument of black and white Marble, Rais'd near
12 Foot from the Ground The Ornaments are fine Foldidge, Feſtoons, & very well don
with a Neat Urn at the Top, and over it the Arms Upon a looſe ſpread Drapery finely
Poliſh'd hanging upon the Baſe this Inſcription following The whole ſecur'd with Iron
Spikes waſh'd with Gold is a curious piece of Workmanſhip and coſt 150 l

H S
THOMAS WINTER *Armiger*
Inclyti illius WINTRI *promptus,*
Qui HISPANORUM *Claſſem*
[*Quæ vinci non putuit*] *fudit*
Belli dein pace Obſtetricante
hic pacis Filius in Indos Mercator Navigat,
Ubi Moſſalapatamæ præfecturam geſſit & adornavit,
Vigiſſimo plus minus anno elapſo
Patri Cognatiſque
(*Ob fidelitatem optimo Regnum a Piris factis ſtoribus*)
ad inopiam reductis)
Felix & Remis Secundis
Plane Alter JOSEPH *mittente rediit,*
Omnibus tandem Boni una functus Officiis

Postquam triginta quatuor Annos
Mirâ patientiâ acri laboraverat morbo,
In Domino moriens à laboribus requievit.

Mæstiſſima Conjux   Obiit Jan 15. ⎰ Salutis MDCLXXXI.
hoc qualecunque Monumentum   ⎱ Ætatis LXVI
Amoris ergo Poſuit.

On a plate of Marble fixt on a Baſe of Portland Stone upon which the Monument ſtands.

Here alſo lyeth *Anne* Daughter of *Richard Swinglehurſt* of *London*
Gentleman Relict of *Thomas Winter* aboveſaid. She Dyed Wife to
Charles Eldeſt Son of Sir *Thomas Orlie* of *Lincolnſhire* Baronet 15 *March*
Anno Domini, 1689. Ætatis ſuæ 54

The Inſcription above in Engliſh.

Here lyes *Thomas Winter* Eſq, the great Grandchild, of that famous *Winter*
who ſhatter'd the Spaniſh Fleet, Stil'd Invincible. The War at laſt
uſhering in Peace, This Son of Peace goes Merchant to The *Indies,*
where with great Honour he diſcharged the Truſt of Governour of
Meſſalapatam. About Twenty Years after he very fortunately Return'd
another *Joſeph* to his Father and Relations, who for their Fidelity to the
beſt of Kings were by the Pious Covenanters Reduc'd to Poverty ;
finally having approv'd himſelf a worthy Man in all Offices, and after
he had for the ſpace of 38 Years Labour'd with Admirable Patience
under a grievous Diſtemper, Died in the Lord, and Reſted from his
Labours.

His ſorrowful Wife as a ſmall   He Died the 15. of *January*
Proof of her Love Erected this   in the Year of our Salvation 1681,
to his Memory.   and in the 66th of his Age.

This Gentleman was deſcended from a Family ever remarkable for their great Bravery
and Valour; his great Grandfather was very famous for the great ſervices done his Country in
Deſtroying the Spaniſh Armado as before, his Grandfather and Father were much eſteem'd
for their Strength and Courage, and his Brother Sir *Edward Winter,* who liv'd at *York* Place
near *Batterſy* the latter part of his Life, (in his Younger Years when a Conſul in *India,*) Kill'd
a *Tyger* with his own Hands without any Weapon. The Story is ſo well known that we need
not add the Particulars

Againſt the South Wall of the Church being the left Hand of the ſaid Iſle.

A Moſt ſtately Monument of black and white Marble ſecur'd with Iron Rails, in all about
14 foot from the Ground done after the Modern Manner, with ſeveral very Elegant Performances in Carving as a neat Drapery, a large Vauſe at the Top, from whence hang Feſtoons, &c and the Arms ſupported by Two wing'd Genii. The whole being an Excell-
lent piece of Workmanſhip perform'd by that great Maſter Mr. *Grin Gibbons,* coſt 300 l

On the Tomb below is this Inſcription;

D. O. M. S.

Beatam hic expectat Reſurrectionem   Deim
DOROTHEA CLARKE   SAMUEL BARROW
Filia & ex Cohæredibus   Ejuſdem Illuſtriſſimi Principis
THOMÆ HYLIARD Huntonienſis,   Medico Ordinario,
ELIZABETHA KYMPTON   Nec non, pro Exercitu Anglicans,
Nupſit Primum   Et Advocato & Judic.,
GULIELMO CLARKE Equiti Aurato,   cum quo
Sereniſſimo Regis Carolo Secundo   ut vixit,
A rebus bellicis Secretario.   Ita ſubtus in pace requieſcit.

Illa Obiit VI Kal   Chariſſima Matri, à cujus uberibus pependit   Illa Obiit 12 Kal
A. D MDCXCV.   Et vitrico optimo, multumque de ſe merito   ap A D MDCLXXXII
                        GEORGE CLARKE
                     Filius unicus & Prrvignus
                              P.

And

And underneath at the Foot of the Tomb is a large black Stone, and on it this.

P. M. S.

Samueles Barrow MD ex vetustâ
In agro Norfolc prosapia
Carolo II. Medici Ordinarii,
Exercitus Anglicano
Advocati Generalis,& Judicis Martialis,
Per annos plus minus viginti;
Quæ munera jussu regio suscepit,
Quod Albemarkum Secutus,
Optatum Caroli red.tum
Suis maturavit consiliis
Uxorem duxit unicam
Relictam Gul Clarke Equit Aur.
Cujus fælicissimi paris
(Annos sexdecim rarum
Amoris Conjuglis exemplum exhibuisset)
Quæ sola potuit, mors fregit Consortium
12 Kal Ap. AD. CIƆIƆCLXXXII.
Infracto adhuc manente superstiris amore.
Obiit Ætatis, LVII.

In English.

Then.

Here lyes expecting a blessed Resurrection *Dorothy Clarke*, Daughter and one of the Co-heirs of *Thomas Hylsard* of *Hampshire* & *Elizabeth Kympton*; she was first Married to Sir *William Clarke* Kt. Secretary of War to his serene Majesty *Charles II.*

Married a Second time to *Sam Barrow* Physician in Ordinary to the same Illustrious Prince, and Judge Advocate of the English Forces, with whom as she liv'd, so underneath Rests peaceably

She Died the 6th. of the Calends of *August Anno Domini,* 1698.

He Dy'd the 12th of the Calends of *April Anno Domini,* 1682

To his Dear Mother on whose Breasts he hung, and to his much and deservedly respected Father in Law , George Clarke, Only Son and Son in Law Erected this Monument.

Then follows

Sacred to the Pious Memory

of *Samuel Barrow* Dr of Physick of an Ancient Family in the County of *Norfolk*, Physician in Ordinary to King *Charles* the II Advocate General and Judge Martial for the space of above 20 Years to the English Army Which Places he took at the Royal Command, bee ink siding with the D of *Albem* By his Faithful Councels he hasten'd the desir'd Return of King *Charles* the Second He Married only one Wife the Relict of Sir *George Clarke* Kt She w is the Wife of an happy pair (and after she had for Sixteen Years given a Singular proof of Conjugal Love) Death, in whose only Power it was at last dissolv'd the Knot the 12th. of the Calends of *April* in the Year 1682 The Love of the Surviver remaining still entire. He Died in the 57 Year of his Age

Near the last

A most Magnificent Monument, I erected to the Memory of *John* Lord *Mordaunt* Viscount *de Avaland* of white and black Marble Design'd thus Upon a large Table of Black Polish'd Marble between 4 and 5 Foot High, supported by a white Pedestal of the same Stone, Stands a Marble Statue of the said Lord, somewhat bigger than the Late m

I is

his Robes, with a Battoon or Staff of Command in his right Hand, as being Conftable of *Windfor* Caftle. 'Tis done with abundance of Spirit by that late Celebrated Englifh Statuary Mr *Bufhnel*, and coft near 250 l His Coronet and Gantlets are fupported by Two Beautiful Stands at each outward Corner of the faid Table, and Two Ovals of white Marble againft the Wall by Two other. The whole Performance is extraordinary Fine, and is computed at 400 l.

Upon his right Hand Oval, is the following Infcription.

H S. I.

Nobiliffimus heros JOHAN MORDAUNT
Johannis Comitis Petroburgenfis
Filius natu minor,
ex
Mordantiorum Stemmate, quod ante fexcentos annos
Normania traductum
Serie perpetua, deinceps hic in Anglia floruit ;
Qui
Acceptum a Parentibus Decus
Rebus Geftis Auxit, & Illuftravit
Opera egregia Pofita
In Reftituendo principe ab avitis Regnis Pulfo,
Mille aditis perieulis,
et
Cromwells Rabie faepius provocata, faepe etiam devicta,
A
Carolo Secundo feliciter Reduce
In laborum mercedem & benevolentiae tefferam
Vice comes de Avisland eft Renunciatus ;
Caftris etiam Windeforiae & Militiae Surrienfis
Praefecturae Admotus ;
ex
Nuptiis cum lectiffima Heroina ELIZABETHA CAREY
Comitum monumethae ftirpe oriunda,
Aufpicatiffime inftis
(Sufcepta prole numerofa)
Filiis Septem Filiabus quatuor ,
Medio Aetatis flore annorum 48 febre correptus,
Vn Immortalitate dignus animam
Deo reddidit
V.
Die Junii Annoque Domini MDCLXXV

On the other Oval follows a very long Pedegree with this Title

Stemma Gentilitium
Mordantiorum
qui
Perannos Sexcentos primum Normannia
deinceps in Anglia Floruerunt

	Osbertus	Mordaunt			
	Miles	Normadia			
	Ofmunus	Mordaunt	Baldwinus		
	Eftachius	Mordaunt	Robertus		
	Gult	Mordaunt	Agnes		
	Guli	Mordaunt	Rich		
Nicholas	Rob	Mordaunt	Guli	Rich.	
	Edmund	Mordaunt			
	Rob.	Mordaunt			
	Rob	Mordaunt	Caffindra		
Matilda	Guli	Mordaunt	Eliz.		
Guil.	Johan	Mordaunt	Eliz.		
Guil.	Johan Miles	Baro. M	Joanna	Rob	
	Johan.	Baro M	Edit.	Anna Marg. Doro. Eliz.	
Winf. Etheld Geor Gul. Edmund	Lodov.	Baro M	Anna.	Urfula	
Mar Eliz.	Han	Baro M	Maria	Eliz	
Kathn					
Joan. Lucy Fran	Johan	Comes. Petro Ludov	Fra Marg.		
Tobian	Han.	Comes. Petro Eliz.			The

The said Infcription in Englifh as followeth:

Here lyes

The Honourable *John Mordaunt*, youngeft Son of *John* Earl of *Peterborough* of the Ancient Stock of the *Mordaunts*, which firft in *Normandy*, and fince in *England* have Flourifh'd for the fpace of 600 Years He took care to improve and advance the Honour of his Family by his Illuftrious Actions, being very Inftrumental in Reftoring the Prince Banifh'd from his Hereditary Dominions, running a Thoufand Dangers: Often provoking, and as often curbing the unbridled rage of *Cromwel* At the happy Reftoration of *Charles* the Second, He was for a Reward of his great Services, and as a publick Teftimony of Royal Favour, created *Vicount de Avriland*, Conftable of *Windfor-Caftle* and Lord Lieutenant of the County of *Surry*. He had by his happy Marriage, with the Noble Lady *Elizabeth Carey* of the Family of the *Monmouths*, a numerous Iffue of Seven Sons and Four-Daughters. Then in the Flower of his Age, in his Forty Eighth Year this Noble Lord being Seiz'd with a Feaver, Refign'd his Soul to God the 5th Day of *June* in the Year of our Lord, 1675.

On the other Oval

The Ancient Family of the *Mordaunts* who have Flourifh'd firft in *Normandy* and fince in *England* for 600 Years.
For the Pedegree, it is fo plain, being nothing but Common Chriftian Names, that we don't think a Tranflation is neceffary

Befides the large Hiftory of this Noble Lord upon his Monument, we think it proper to add, that in his Younger Years, he was very Active in raifing Men for the Service of his Majefty King *Charles* I under the Earl of *Holland*, with Defign to have fet that Prince at Liberty when Confin'd by the Parliament in the Ifle of Wight His Eldeft Son *Charles*, who fucceeded him in his Honours, was very Inftrumental in the late Revolution in 1688, and was by King *William* created Earl of *Monmouth*, into which Honourable Family his faid Father Married Afterwards he had the Title of Earl of *Peterborough* devolv'd upon him by the Death of *Henry Mordaunt* his Uncle, Earl of that place, and is by her Majefty, in confideration of his great Experience, Courage, and known Loyalty, made General of her Forces now in *Catalonia*, under whofe Conduct *Barcelona* the Capital City, and that whole Province is already Reduc'd by 'em to the Obedience of King *Charles* III.

Between the laft Two Monuments

Is an Ancient performance to the Memory of Mrs *Katharine Hart*, in which She and her Two Sons, and Two Daughters are reprefented Kneeling after the Old Manner She Dyed in the Year 1605, and lyeth buried hard by

A Monument of Alabafter about 8 Foot High, Gilded, Painted and Adorn'd with Antique Imbelfhment, having the Figures of *William Payne* Efq, and his Wife kneeling before in Altar, and underneath this Infcription,

William Payne of *Pallingfwick* Efq, to the Memory of himfelf and *Jane* his Wife, who lived with him in Wedlock 44 Years, and dyed the firft Day of *May*, *Anno Domini*, 1610 and the faid *William* died the   day of   *Anno Dom*   the faid *William Payne* hath given for ever their his Deceafe an Ifland in the River of *Thames* called *Muckenfh w* to the ufe of the Poor of this Parifh on *Hammerfmith Side*

A Beautiful Monument of Marble of feveral Colours, about 10 Foot in length From a neat Urn above having neat Feftoons, &c. Over the Infcription is Two Cherubs heads fupporting the Arms

Here lyeth the Body of Sir *Thomas Kinfey* Kt and Alderman of the City of *London*, who Dy'd the 3d Day of *Jan* in the Year of our Lord 1696 and in the 60th Year of his Age
And a confiderable diftance lower (Room being left for another Infcrip on) follows.
In the fame Grave lye alfo the Bodies of ROBERT and ELIZABETH Atkins, his Grandchildren by his only Child *Mary* the Wife of *Richard Atkins* Efquire

In the Pavement about the Middle of the Ifle is a Plain black Stone, and upon it this Inscription.

P. M. S.

Sub certâ fpe Refurgendi repoftæ
Hic jacent Reliquiæ
Humphredi Henchman Londinenfis Epifcopi,
Et Gravitate & paftorali Clementiâ,
(Quæ vel in vultu Elucebant)
Et vitæ etiam Sanctitate Venerabilis
Spectatâ in Ecclefiam afflictam Conftantiâ,
Singulari in Regem periclitantem Fide,
Quo feliciter reftituto,
Cùm Sarisburienfi Diæcefi duos Annos
Londinenfi duodecim præfuiffet
Regi etiam ab Eleemofynis & Sanctioribus Confiliis,
Plenus Annis, & Cupiens diffolvi,
Obdormivit in Domino.

Octob. 7. Anno $\begin{cases} Dom \; 1675. \\ Ætat \; 83 \end{cases}$

Redemptor meus vivit.

In Englifh thus.

Sacred to the Pious Memory

In affured hope of the Refurrection, here lyes the Afhes of *Hum Henchman* Bifhop of *London,* Venerable for his Gravity and paftoral Clemency, (Legible in his very Countenance) and alfo for the Sanctity of his Life. He was of well try'd Conftancy to the oppreffed Church, of fingular Loyalty to the King, when in the greateft Hazards; after whofe happy Reftoration he was firft made Bifhop of *Salisbury* where he continued Two Years. Afterwards tranflated to the See of *London,* where he remain'd Twelve Years. He was alfo made the Kings Almoner, and a Privy Councellour . being full of Years and longing for his Diffolution. He fell Afleep in the Lord.

The 7th. of Octob. $\begin{cases} \text{in the Year of Grace } 1675 \\ \text{of his Age} \text{———} 83. \end{cases}$

My Redeemer liveth.

The Character of this Pious and Reverend Prelate here given, is fo Juft and Adequate to his Life and Actions, and fo admirably and comprehensively Compos'd, that there feems no Room to add any thing, except of his Charity and Hofpitality, which were fo great that fome Part of the Town of *Fulham* fubfifted upon the Bounty of his overflowing Table, where in Time of need they always were certainly Supply'd. And fo great is the Veneration, they have for his Memory, that feveral who knew him, can't Mention his Name, even now, without unufual Concern

A Plain Alabafter Monument at the Weft End of the faid Ifle with this Infcription

In Memory of *William Earfby* of *Northend* Gent who departed this Life the 18. of *Octob.* 1664 Aged 73
And in the Pavement under a black Stone lyeth *John Earfby* his Son, of the fame Place Gent who Dyed *Septem.* 9th. 1687. Aged 47 Years, alfo *Mary* his Wife who Dyed *Jan.* 11th 1690 Aged alfo 47
Near them alfo lyeth their Daughter *Martha,* Wife of *Edward Bullingby* of *Weftminfter* Gentleman, who dyed *Anno Domini* 1698 Aged 26 Years.

In the Pavement of the Middle Ifle.

On a large black Stone this Inſcription.

Here lyes the Body of *Elizabeth Tipping*, Daughter of *Edward* ------- of *Hilleſley* in the County of *Gloceſter* Eſq, by his Wife *Frances* eldeſt Daughter of *William Tyre* of *Hardwickcourt* in *Hardwick* in the ſaid County Eſq, Deſcended from one of the Coheireſſes of Sir *Charles Brandon* Knight Duke of *Suffolk*, Knight of the moſt Noble Order of the Garter, having Iſſue *Lucretia* one only Daughter by her Husband. Deceaſed 29 *July* 1686 Aged 22 Years

On a large black Stone.

M S.

Here lyeth the Body of *Robert Hick.* Eſq, who Dyed the 23d. of *June* 1669. *Ætatis Suæ* 56

Reſurrecturus

On another

Here lyeth the Body of *Robert Blanchard* Citizen and Goldſmith of *London*, and an Inhabitant of this Pariſh, who Dyed the 6th. Day of *June Annoque Domini*, 1680 *Ætatis Suæ* 57

In the North Iſle, at the Weſt End

Is a very handſome Monument of white Marble, Secur'd with Iron Rails, beautified with a neat Border of Carving Fruit, Flowers, &c. and on it this Inſcription.

Here lyes Buried *Eliz. Limpany* Daughter of *Robert* and *Iſabel Limpany*, who Dyed *October* the 10th 1694 and in the 3d. Year of her Age
This Monument Coſt 100 Pound.

In the Middle of the Iſle, a ſmall Marble Monument.

Near this Place lyes Interr'd the Body of *Abraham Downing* Eſq, Sergeant Skinner to his Majeſty *Charles* II. He Married *Anne* the Daughter of *William Prew* Rector of *Ditton* in *Kent*, and had by her Four Children, *Richard* now living, and *William, Prudence* and *Anne*, Buried near this Place He departed this Life *January* the 19, 1676 Aged 59 Years

There are ſeveral other Stones of Perſons of no Note, in and about this Church which we thought not fit to inſert.

Of the ADVOWSON

The Right of Preſentation to this Living is now in *James Bridges* Eſq, who lately Purchas'd it with the great Tythes of the Lady *Elwes* Widow of Sir *John Elwes* lately Dead, is alſo an Eſtate in this Pariſh, and a fine Ancient Seat by the *Thames* Side call'd Grove Houſe. The Reverend Mr *William Barry* is Vicar of this Pariſh This Vicarage is valued in the Queens Book at Ten Pound *Per Annum*, but is thought worth about 150 Pound

The TOWN

This Town is conveniently and pleaſantly ſituated, tho' in the Opinion of ſome not very healthful, great part of the Buildings ſtanding upon a wet moiſt ſort of Ground It has been a Place much frequented formerly by the Nobility and Gentry, and noted for ſeveral good Seats, particularly one (which by the Building appears very Ancient,) belonging now to the See of *London*, where the preſent Biſhop, the Honourable and Venerable Dr *Hen Compton* generally Reſides, as moſt of his Predeceſſors uſed to do, tho' this Houſe formerly ſeem'd to belong to the Crown from this Paſſage of *Norden* [*Speculum Brit*] There is an Ancient Houſe belonging to the See of *London* united about *Henry* III often lay it this Place The Antiquity, Buildings and priſtine Eſtate of this Village will further appear from *I ind*, who ſays [*Cygnea Cantio*] D mai

————Domus Volucrum
Tum frontem erexit ante multa fæcla
Danis cognita villa bellicofis,
Quam dum fufpicio lubens micantem
Amplis Nobilium ædibus virorum.

This fhews how it Flourifh'd in and before the time he Writ, which was in the Reign of.
Henry VIII.

Then fpeaking [*In Notis*] of the Bifhops Houfe there he fays

————Volucrum Domus Saxoniæ Fulenham Vulgo Fulham Afferius menevenfis fcribit Danorum turmas hâc ripa in hybernis fuiffe. Fuit hæc villa multis abhinc annis atque adeo nunc eft hofpitio Londinenfis Epifcopi notiffima.

So that ev'n then 'twas call'd the Old Seat of the Bifhop of *London*. But that which is the moft remarkable Inftance of it's Antiquity, and made it well known in Hiftory, long before the Conqueft, is, that 'twas here the Army of the *Pagan Danes* Encamp'd in the time of *Alphred* King of the Weft *Saxons, Anno Domini* 879. after they had Burnt, Ravag'd and Deftroy'd almoft all the Towns in *England*, and left nothing but Ruin and Defolation behind them, they took up their Winter Quarters here, the Woods, and Apt Situation of the Place (fays *Norden*) [*Spec Brit.*] for paffage by Water, no doubt moved them thereunto, and after they had ftaid till the Return of the Spring, they broke up, Crofs'd the Sea, and Encamp'd near *Ghent* in *Flanders*, from thence call'd *Frone-land* where they continued a Year longer

It feems at Prefent to be in a declining and languifhing Condition, not but it boaft's of a greater Number of Houfes, and Inhabitants than was known in it formerly, but the Buildings are not fo Magnificent as chofe more Antient, nor is here the many Honourable and Worthy Families, at prefent which us'd to refide upon this Spot. It has been much Augmented in Number of Houfes of late for the Dwellings of the Tradefmen, and fuch as live by their Labour, who are chiefly Gardeners, Farmers, Husbandmen and Watermen, not that it wants good Edifices and Confiderable Families to Enoble it as will appear by and by The Houfes of the Common People are commonly neat and well Built of Brick, and from the Gate of the Queens Road run along on both Sides of the Way almoft as far as the Church Alfo from the *Thames* Side into the Town ftands an entire Range of Buildings, and upon the Paffage leading to the Church call'd Church Lane, are feveral very Handfom Airy Houfes But the Buildings of this place run furtheft toward the North, extending themfelves in a Street, through which lyes the Road a very Confiderable way towards *Hammerfmith*, befides there are feveral other handfome Buildings towards the Eaft call'd the back Lane, and a great Number of Gardeners Houfes fcatter'd in the feveral remote Parts of the Parifh This Place being fo conveniently feated both for Paffage to *London*, and the Pleafure of its Walks, is fill'd during the Summer Seafon with Abundance of Citizens and Confiderable Perfons, where (as at its Neighbour *Putney* and feveral other *Villages* upon the *Thames*,) they are handfomely accommodated with good Lodgings to the great Advantage of the Inhabitants

Of the Seats and moft confiderable Inhabitants, &c

1 THE Houfe of my Lord of *London*, before mention'd, ftands near the Church very pleafuntly feated, having a View on the River *Thames*, and a private pair of Stairs to take the Water at This Houfe being of a very Confiderable ftanding, and having been often Repair'd, Alter'd, and had Additions made to it fince its firft Building, does not appear fo Regular and Beautiful as more Modern Buildings, however the many Conveniencies in it make amends for its want of outward Ornament It has a very Choice Library, which has been much Augmented by the Bounty of the prefent Bifhop. But that which in the Opinion of the Inhabitants renders it moft Valuable, is the Bountiful Houfe-keeping in it, and the Charity they often Receive from it in their Neceffity The Gardens Round this Houfe as they are now improv'd by his Lordfhip, are very Fine and Entertaining, and the kindnefs of the Soyle and great Plenty of Water makes them very proper for the Breeding of fome Choice foreign Plants, of which here is a very valuable Collection. There is likewife a fmall Park adjoyning, which (with the Gardens, &c) is moated all Round by a large Canal well Stor'd with Fifh, in and upon the Banks of which are Five or Six Choice Phyfical Plants found, not Difcover'd to Grow naturally in any other Part of *England* [*Camdens Brit pa* 336, 337]

2 Upon the *Thames* adjoyning to *Hammafmith*, tho' within the limits of *Fulham* Divifion is a Noble Seat Built by Sir *Nicholas Crisp* Baronet, a Gent of Unfhaken Loyalty to King *Charles* I It ftands a very convenient Diftance from the *Thames* in a Sweet and Wholfome Air, and has a large Spot of Ground of feveral Acres Inclos'd, adjoyning to it The Building is
very

very lofty, Regular, and Magnificent, after the Modern Manner, Built of Brick, Corner'd with Stone, and has a handſom Cupola at the Top. It contains ſeveral very handſome Rooms very ſpacious and finely Finiſh'd. The Foundations and Walls are very Subſtantial, and the Vaults underneath Arch'd in an Extraordinary Manner. The whole Houſe in Building, and the Gardens, Canalls &c. in Making, is ſaid to Coſt near Three and Twenty Thouſand Pounds. Some time after the Death of the ſaid Sir *Nicholas*, this Houſe was Sold to Mrs *Margaret Hews* a Lady much Eſteem'd at Court about that time, for her Air and Beauty, in whoſe Poſſeſſion it had not Remain'd many Years before ſhe Diſpos'd of it again to ------- *Lenoy* Eſq, one of her Majeſties Juſtices of the Peace for this County, and Mr ----- *Tredway* his Brother, both Turkey Merchants, Gentlemen of known Worth is well Abroad as at Home. Theſe Gentlemen have for many Years paſt liv'd in this Noble Seat, and made ſeveral other Buildings as Dyehouſes, &c. for the carrying on of their Buſineſs here

3 A very Ancient Seat Situate upon the *Thames* towards the Weſt Limits of this Pariſh near *Chelſea*, call'd *Grove* Houſe, lately the Seat of Sir *John Elwes* Deceas'd, a Juſtice of Peace for this County, and before of *Henry Elwes* Eſq, his Uncle, but now Purchas'd with the Great Tythes, and a fine Eſtate adjoyning by ------ *Bridges* Eſq. This Seat is ſweetly ſituated, and is very Pleaſant in Summer, tho' in Winter 'tis ſometimes incommoded by the Water, being upon a low Ground. The Gardens are extraordinary Fine, and the many Winter Greens; as *Cypreſs*, *Yew*, and *Fir*, which Flouriſh here extreamly, make it very Remarkable.

4 In the Road going towards *Walham Green* ſomewhat North Eaſt of the Town, is a handſome Antient Houſe belonging to Sir *Joſeph Williams*, or his Son *Joſeph Williams* Eſq, Mr *March* Chirurgeon lives here at preſent. There is alſo Two or Three other handſome Houſes adjoyning, whoſe Inhabitants don't readily occur to our Memory

5 At the Eaſt Entrance of this Town by the Queens Gate, is a Neat convenient Houſe of Captain *Woodward*, one of her Majeſties Juſtices of the Peace for *Middleſex*, 'tis but ſmall, but very well contriv'd, his Gardens alſo are very handſome.

I In this Pariſh are Scatter'd ſeveral large Villages, as *Parſons-Green* to the Eaſt of this Town ſituate upon the long Road, Inhabited moſtly by Gentry, and Perſons of Quality, and has ſeveral very handſome Houſes, all ſtanding very Airy upon a Dry Clean Green, viz

6 A Seat of Sir *Francis Child* Alderman and late Lord Mayor of *London*; well Built with Brick after the Modern Manner, and looks very ſtately, the Gardens alſo are very good

7 Another adjoyning, in which dwells Mr *Poultney* a Turkey Merchant, this s a large regular new built brick Houſe, and is made very Convenient. There is alſo Two or Three other very handſome Seats here, which we can't now particularize, becauſe we muſt give ſome Account of an Ancient Seat belonging to the Right Honourable the Earl of *Peterborough*

This Seat is a very large Square, Regular Pile built of Brick, and has a Gallery all round it upon the Roof. 'Twas built by a Branch of the Honourable Family of the *Monmouths*, and came to the Preſent Earl in Right of his Mother, the Lady *Elizabeth Carey* Viſcounteſs *De Aviland*. It has abundance of extraordinary good Rooms with fine Painting &c. but is moſtly Remarkable for it's ſpacious Gardens, there being above Twenty Acres of Ground Incloſ'd. The Contrivance of the Ground is fine, tho' their Beauty is in a great Meaſure Decay'd. And the large Cypreſs Shades and Pleaſant Wildernſſes, with Fountains, Statues, &c. have been very entertaining. In this Garden is a natural Curioſity, not to be paralleld (as is ſaid) in *Europe* viz a Tree which bears a Yellow Tulip of 70 Foot High, and it's Stem about 5 Foot 9 Inches in Circumference. It is of almoſt 60 Years Growth, has a ſmooth Gray ſort of a Coat, and a very fine green Leaf

II. Some little diſtance North-eaſt is *Walham Green*, a Village in which lives a very conſiderable number of People, moſt Gardeners, whoſe Kitchin, Greens, Plants, Herbs, Roots and Flowers daily ſupply *Weſtminſter* and *Covent-Garden* Markets, here are no Houſes of any conſiderable Note

III *North-end* a ſmall but Pleaſant Airy Village, inhabited moſtly by Gardeners, at this Place was a good Houſe belonging to the Family of the *Fanſby s*, who for many Years have reſided here

IV There is alſo a ſmall Village call'd *Broome-houſe*, near the *Thames* Eaſt of *Fulham*, and part of *Sand end* before Mention'd, at which laſt Place is a Work Houſe, for making of that very uſeful Manufactury of Sail Cloath, where ſometimes Seventy or Eighty Hands are Imploy'd.

The Mannor in this Pariſh belongs to the See of *London*

STanding about a Mile North-eaſt from *Fulham* ; called in Doomeſday Book *Hermoderwode,* and in an Antient deed in the Exchequer, *Hermoderworth,* which is an evidence of its Antiquity, becauſe 'twas in that time a place well known. We ſhall not attempt accounting for the preſent Name of it *Hammerſmith,* which is ſomewhat odd, unleſs ſuppoſing Time has melted thoſe rough *Saxon* Sounds will do, which indeed ſeems more probable, than ſeveral Conjectures we heard about it, or that ridiculous Account firmly believed by ſome of the Inhabitants of *Fulham* and *Putney,* as well as of this Place, *viz.* that the Two Churches, of the Two firſt nam'd Places, were many Ages ſince Built by Two Siſters of Gigantick Stature, who had but one Hammer between them, which they us'd to throw over the River, from one to another when they wanted it, but one time in its fall it happen'd unfortunately upon its Clawes and broke them, ſo that the pious Work muſt unavoidably have ſtood ſtill if they could not have got it mended ; but going to a Smith that liv'd at this Place, he ſet all to rights again, and for ſuch a publick Piece of Service, it has ever ſince retain'd the name of *Hammerſmith*   This fantaſtick Relation is incerted only for the Readers Diverſion, and to let him ſee the force of Tradition, and how ſtrangely the Ignorant may be Impos'd upon, eſpecially if there is the leaſt Shadow of Truth to ſupport it, as there is here, the Towers of the Two Churches being exactly alike, and proportionable (tho' *Fulham* is the largeſt,) built of the ſame Stone, and by the Condition of both, about the ſame time, and then the name of *Hammerſmith* colours the whole Story admirably well, and puts its certainty (with them) out of Doubt

This Village is Situated upon the *Thames,* and extends it ſelf North, as far as the great Weſtern Road, and has ſeveral good Houſes in and about it, inhabited by Gentry and Perſons of Quality, and for above an Hundred Years paſt has been a Summer Retreat for Nobility and Wealthy Citizens, eſpecially from about the Years 1620 and the late unnatural Rebellion, as will appear by and by   It ſtands within the Pariſh of *Fulham* as before, (to which Church, this Chappel here is a Chappel of Eaſe) therefore its Bounds are already taken Notice of in that Pariſh, and conſequently its whole limits known, when the Reader is acquainted, where 'tis divided Eaſtward from *Fulham,* which Diviſion begins at the *Thames* a little to the Eaſt of this Place, and runs irregularly towards the North and North Eaſt, as far as the Pariſh of *Acton.* The Cauſes of the ſaid Diviſion, are next to be conſider'd, as alſo ſome Account of the Chappel.

THE CHAPPEL

THE very Name of a Chappel of Eaſe ſufficiently Points out the Cauſes of its Erection, and indeed the great Number of People inhabiting in and near this Place, at ſuch a great diſtance from *Fulham* Church made the erecting of a Chappel long Deſir'd, and talk'd of, before it could be effected, but about the Year 1624, the great number of Gentry reſiding here, being ſenſible of the Inconveniences, as well as the poorer People, began in earneſt to think of this Remedy, and after ſeveral of them had largely Subſcrib'd they ſet about the Work with all poſſible Application   The whole Number of Inhabitants, who were willing to enjoy the benefit of this Chappel, voluntarily Subſcrib'd, and were included within the limits belonging to it upon the Diviſion, ſo that a very Conſiderable Sum was Secur'd   The limits of this Chappel was divided from *Fulham* before the Year 1622, as appears by a Benefaction to the Poor of *Fulham* in the Table at the End   About the Year 1628, the Foundation of the Chappel was laid, and the Building was carried on with ſuch Expedition, that in the Year 1631 'twas compleatly finiſh'd and conſecrated, tho' it the Weſt end there is a Stone fixt in the Wall with this Date 1630, which was placed there, when the ſaid End was Built, probably before the Inſide was begun   The whole building is of Brick, very ſpatious and regular, and at the Eaſt End is a large ſquare Tower of the ſame, with a ring of Six Bells   The inſide is very well Finiſh'd, being beautified with ſeveral devices in painting   The Cieling alſo is very neatly painted, and in ſeveral Compartments and Ovals were finely depicted the Arms of *England,* alſo Roſes, Thiſtles, Flower-de-luces, &c. all of which the Rebells in their furious Zeal daſh'd out, or daub'd over, tho' this particular Act was more the Effect of their Malice againſt his Majeſty King *Charles I* and the ſacred Kingly Office, than their blind Zeal againſt Popery, endeavouring to the utmoſt, that the Memory of a King ſhould be Expung'd the World   The Glaſs of the Chancel Window was alſo finely painted with *Moſes, Aaron &c.* alſo the Arms of the moſt conſiderable Benefactors, but theſe have been much abus'd (probably by the ſame ungodly Crew, as Relicks of Popery and Superſtition,) however the remains of them evince their former Art and Beauty, which was very Extraordinary   In ſeveral of the other Windows likewiſe there are the Benefactors Coats of Arms, particularly Sir *Nicholas Crispe,* who may be call'd its Founder, himſelf giving in Money and Materials the Sum of Seven Hundred Pounds towards its Building   'Twis likewiſe very well Pav'd, and Pew'd with Wainſcot, and made commodious and beautiful within, as well as ſtately without, the whole charge of which was

was about Two Thousand and odd Pounds   Besides this, ample Provision was made for the
Minister, &c. of which in its proper Place   Notwithstanding the ill usages this Chappel has
met with, 'tis still in very good Condition, besides it is adorn'd with several stately Monu
ments now standing.

The Monuments and Inscriptions

In the Chancel stands Two or Three very   stately ones viz On the right Hand
against the Wall

A Tomb of black and white Marble about Seven Foot long, Three Foot high, and Three
Foot over, defended with Iron Rails, and on a very neat Monument of the same placed
above it, is Inscrib'd as followeth.

TO THE LASTING MEMORY

Of the right Honourable *Edmund* Lord *Sheffield* Earl of *Mulgrave*,
Baron of *Butterwick*, and Knight of the most Noble Order of the
Garter. Which Honour of the Garter was conferr'd on him by
Queen *Elizabeth*, for his valiant Services in 88 against the
Spaniard He being then Captain of the Ship call'd the Bear,
and Commander of a Squadron of Ships After that he serv'd
her Majesty in the Irish Wars, where God so blessed him, that
he gain'd much Honour
By King *James* he was made President of the North, where
he Govern'd many Years, with such Integrity, that Injustice
was never laid to his Charge
He was a good Patron to his Country, endeavouring to Advance the Church and Common Wealth He was truly Pious,
open handed to feed the Poor, and Cloath the Naked As he
liv'd the Life, so he dy'd the Death of the Righteous, on
October MDCXLVI in the 83d Year of his Age, and lyeth here
under Interred
The Vertuous Pious and truly Noble Lady *Mariana* Countess
of *Mulgrave*, his dearly beloved Wife surviving him, in Expression
of her Conjugal Love erected this Monument
D   S   P   F.   C
Underneath upon the Tomb
The Lady *Sheffield* repaired this Monument *Anno Domini*, 1682

The Character of this Noble Peer here Interr'd is very well known to all, who are acquainted
with our History, as far as a Century past His Grandson *John* Succeeds him not only
in his Title, but was created Marquess of *Normanby* by King *Charles* II and Duke of
Buckinghamshire by her present Majesty, having by his great Parts, faithful Councel and
stedfast adherence to the true Interest of his Country, justly merited the Character of a
great Statesman and Zealous Patriot.

On the left hand against the Wall.

A very stately Monument of black and white Marble secur'd with Iron Spikes, at the
bottom is a Tomb of Seven Foot Long, Three Foot High, and about Two Foot and an
half over, Cover'd with a polish'd Stone of black Marble Upon which stands the Monu
ment about Six Foot High, in form Triangular Upon the Top of which, is the Head of
Alderman *Smith* well done with Two Alabaster Figures Weeping Upon a Table of black
Marble, is thus Inscrib'd in Letters of Gold

To the lasting Memory of *James Smith* Esq, Citizen and Salter,
and sometimes Alderman of the City of *London*, who Fin'd
Also for the Office of Sheriff, and was one of the Governors
of *Christ's* Hospital of the said City A good Benefactor to
his Country, in Erecting Alm Houses for the Relief of the Poor
in the Parish of *Cookham* near *Maidenhead*, where he was Born
He was also very Liberal to the Children of *Christ's* Hospital,
and to the said Company of *Salters*, and very free in many other
Charitable uses for the good of the Poor He had the blessing
of many Children, whereof I ave, by *Mary* his first Wife deceased,

and by his Second Wife *Sarah* now living Fifteen, who out of Love to her deceased Husband hath erected this Monument He Dy'd the 10th. of *October*, 1667 and in the 80th Year of his Age.

And underneath upon the Tomb thus

Here also lyeth the Body of *Sarah Smith* Widow of the abovesaid *James Smith*, the only Daughter of *Robert Cotton* late of *West-Barge-holt* in the County of *Essex* Gentleman deceased, and one truly Joyn'd to her Husband, not only in Conjugal Love, but also in bountiful Charity, having lately augmented the Gifts of her late Husband, and then changed this Life the 29th. of *January* 168 and in the 76th Year of her Age

'Tis said several of their Children and Family lye Interr'd here with them

Near the last towards the left Hand, is placed, a considerable Height from the Ground, a large Alabaster Monument, near Nine Foot in Length, Embellish'd with Gilding and Flowers, *&c* and upon a black Stone thus Written.

Near this place resteth in Expectation of a glorious Resurrection the Mortal part of Mrs. *Mary Green,* Daughter of *Edward Tursel* Esq, and Wife of *John Green* of *London* Merchant, who dyed in Childbed the 23d of *November*, 1657 Aged Seventeen, leaving behind her one Son For whose pious Memory her Husband erected this Monument.

> *Fæmina chara viro, superis dilecta, parentum*
> *Deliciæ, rapidâ Morte perempta jacet,*
> *Quæ famam meritis superavit, moribus annos,*
> *Et Sexum ingenio, & religione suam*
> *Gemmam hanc ostendit mundo natura, sed illam,*
> *Indigno rapuit, Cælicolisque dedit.*
> *Sit brevis in Terra quamvis mora nu puta*
> *Vitam quæ Fuerat non nisi sancta brevem*
>   *ETIAM post Funera vivit,*
>   *In Suorum Desideriis*
>   *In Bonorum Præconiis*
>   *In Cælorum Gaudiis*

And then follows Six Latin Verses, but so Decay'd that we could not pick some out of them, wherefore we thought it proper wholly to omit them.

The foregoing Inscriptions

In English thus.

Here lyes a Woman Snatch't by sudden Death
Dear to her Husband, and by Heavens Belov'd,
The sole Delight and Comfort of her Parents
Whose Merit Fame out-stript, Prudence her Years
In Wit and Vertue, [*went beyond) her Sex.   * or, she excell'd her Sex
Nature just shew'd this Jewel to the World
Then, as if 'twas not Worthy to Enjoy her
Took her away with an officious haste
And straight Convey'd her to Cælestial Bliss

Tho' buried still she Lives
In the Desires of her Friends;
In the Praises of good Men,
And in the Joys of Heaven

On

On a plain Stone adjoyning a good diſtance from the Ground, with ſeveral antient Ornaments round it are theſe Words.

Poſt ⎰ *Tenebras lucem*
⎱ *Pugnam Pacem*
⎰ *Vulnera Vitam*

Heìc latet Franciſcus Wolley, patris Edvards D. D Theologiæ, &
Mariæ Matris Filius Obſequentiſſimus Medis Templi Londini Alumnus.
In Terram Cecidit Decimo Septimo Die Menſis Januarii, Annoque Dom.
MDCLIX.
In Gremio matris cineres requieſcite: Cæli Dum tuba de geliâ vos re-
vocabit humo, cras nos iterabimus.

Edvardus ⎰
Maria ⎬ Wolley *ſine teſte dolentes.*
Jana ⎱

In Engliſh thus

Darkneſs ſucceeds light,
Peace War
and Life follows Death.

Here lyes *Francis Wolley,* the moſt Dutiful and Obedient Son of
Edward and *Mary Wolley,* Dr in Divinity. Student of the
Middle Temple *London.* He died the 17th of *January* in the
Year of our Lord, 1659.
Reſt Aſhes in your Mothers Arms, till Heavens great Trump
ſhall call you up. To morrow we'll repeat our Wiſhes.

Edward ⎰
Mary ⎬ *Wolley.*
Jane ⎱

On a plain black Stone in the Chancel Pavement is this Inſcription.

DEPOSITUM
Radolphi Box militis, Qui Obiit XXIII *die Martii, Anno Domini,*
MDCXCIII.
Ætatis ſuæ LXVII.
E T
Elizabetha Uxoris Ejus, Quæ Obiit XXV. *die Jan. Anno Domini,*
MDCXCIII.
Ætatis Suæ LIV.

In Engliſh thus.

Here lyeth the Body of Sir *Ralph Box* Knight, who Dy'd the 23d.
of *March,* in the Year of our Lord 1693 Aged 67. As alſo of
Elizabeth his Wife, who Dy'd the 25th. Day of *January,* in the
Year of our Lord 1693 Aged 54.

On another Stone lying even with the former is a Coat neatly done and a Marqs. *Coronet,*
with this Inſcription.

D. O. M. S
Nobiliſſimo Illuſtriſſimoque viro LUDOVICO DE *SAINT DELIS,*
MARCHIONI DE HEUCOURT,
Natione Gallo,
Fide Sincerâ,
Pietate Eximiâ,
Probitate Singulari
Conſpicuo,
morum amænitate amabili,
Relictis quas amplas habebat Opibus,
Religionis Cauſâ in Anglia Profugo,

M

ELIZABETHA
Nobileſſima LE, COMITE, DE NOMANT
Familiâ Oriunda
Uxor Moerens
H. M. P. C
Vixit Annos LXVII.
Objit Die Decembris **XVII**
Anno Domini MDCXCIII.

To the Noble and Illuſtrious *Lewis de Saint Deliſs Marquiſs de Heucourt* by Birth a Frenchman, of ſtedfaſt Loyalty, Extraordinary Piety, ſingular Honeſty, and Remarkable for his Candour and Affability. Who left what Poſſeſſions he had, which were very Conſiderable, and retired to *England* for the ſake of his Religion *Elizabeth* of the Noble Family of the Count *de Nomant*, his ſorrowful Lady Dedicated this Marble He Liv'd 72 Years, and died the 6th. of *December*, in the Year of our Lord 1698.

This Nobleman brought with him a Sufficiency from his Native Country, not only to ſupport the Dignity of his Title, but alſo to relieve the Neceſſities of his Poor Countrymen, which he always very liberally did, and died in an Old Age very much lamented

At the South-eaſt Corner of this Chappel, and very near the Pulpit, rais'd a conſiderable diſtance from the Ground, is a Neat Monument of black and white Marble, near Eight Foot long, and about Two Broad, upon which is a braſs Head of King *Charles* the I and underneath it in an Oval is Written thus

This Effigies was Erected by the ſpecial Appointment of Sir *Nicholas Criſpe* Knight and Baronet, as a grateful Commemoration of that Glorious Martyr King *Charles* I. of bleſſed Memory

And under the ſaid Oval a ſmall white Marble Urne, upon a black Pedeſtal, on which is Inſcrib'd as followeth.

Within this Urne is Entomb'd the Heart of Sir *Nicholas Criſpe* Kt. and Baronet, a Loyal Sharer in the Sufferings of his late and preſent Majeſty. He firſt ſetled the Trade of Gold from *Gunea*, and there Built the Caſtle of *Cormantine*. Died the 26th. of *February* 1665. Aged 67

The Yearly Value of this Living is about 142 l. *Per Annum*, and ariſeth from the Rent or Rates of the Seats, and Pews which the Inhabitants of *Hammerſmith* Pay, beſides their Pariſh Duties to *Fulham*

The Miniſter of *Hammerſmith* is Choſen by the Inhabitants of the liberty thereof, and is the Reverend Mr. *John Wade*, who has for many Years paſt been in this Cure.

Of the Buildings

This Village having within the Circle of 80 or 90 Years paſt been much frequented by wealthy Perſons, it has in that time much Flouriſh'd in Buildings, and is from a Poor Contemptible Village Swell'd into a large well Built Place, which for bigneſs deſerves the Name of a Town, which we ſhall therefore uſe as we have done (before tho' improperly) for the other Villages already Touch'd upon, Cuſtom in ſome Meaſure giving us this Liberty It being ſeated upon the Weſtern Road, and having a large Hoſpital, made it formerly be taken Notice of, and the general Reputation for its healthfulneſs, and the Commodious Paſſage to *London* by Water, or otherwiſe has made it lately Flouriſh Upon a careful ſurvey of the Adjoyning ſeats, there ſeems none of above 100 Years ſtanding, ſo that whatever there might formerly be, they were long ſince Demoliſh'd, or raz'd, when this Place began to be in Eſteem, to make way for the ſeveral Modern Houſes now ſtanding If we obſerve likewiſe the Tradeſmens Houſes in this Place, we ſhall find few of them Ancienter than the Time before mention'd, and moſt of them Built not above 50 Years, ſo that this Place ſtood it a ſtand a long time, but has extreamly Flouriſh'd within 10 or 12 Years paſt, perhaps its Vicinity to *Kenſington* being no ſmall Cauſe, It extends it ſelf a very great length from *Kenſington*, in the Eaſt, to *Turnham Green* in the Weſt, and has Houſes very Thick on both ſides the Way, ſo that the Road ſeems a long Street. It has Two Rows of Buildings run down from the

the Chappel to the *Thames* Side, and then shoots it self upon the Banks thereof, in a very stately manner near half a Mile towards *Chifwick* Amongst this Row of stately Houses one was thought Magnificent enough to entertain Queen *Katherine*, now Queen *Dowager*, where she kept her Palace in Summer time. Several other Noble Persons have Liv'd here, and in the Neighbourhood. The most Eminent that at present reside upon this Spot follow

The Seats and Confiderable Inhabitants.

IN a very handsome Seat fronting the *Thames* lately dwelt *Nevill* one of the Barons of her Majesties Exchequer, who some Months since died there.

In the House where Queen *Dowager* before Mention'd Liv'd, now Dwells Mr. *Henry Nash* Gent

At a handsome House fronting the Chappel　　　 *Fern* Esq,

Here also dwells in very handsome Seats hard by Mr. *Halley* Esq, also *Nich Goodwin* Esq; both Justices of the Peace for the County of *Middlesex*, and Mr *John Wade.*

Formerly here stood an Hospital in this Place above the Creek, [*Norden Sp Brit*] but not a Stone nor so much as the Remembrance of it, is now left

This Town depends much upon the Road, and has a very great Number of Alehouses and Places of Entertainment Also Shopkeepers and retailers of several Commodities, but the greatest part of the Inhabitants are Gardeners, Watermen, Fishermen, and Persons that get their Bread by their Day Labour

CHISWICK.

NExt we meet with upon the *Thames* is the pleasant village of *Chifwick*, situate about Three Miles by the *Thames* side from *Fulham*, and Eight from *London*, was anciently called *Chefewitk* as appears in Doomesday Book, and some very old Deeds.

The Sweet Air and Situation of this Place, drew not only a great many confiderable Families to settle here formerly, but induc'd several Illustrious Persons to build Seats, nor has it lost its Reputation now, but is Honoured with the Presence of several noble Persons. Altho' we find no mention made of this Place in History, yet several very ancient Buildings now standing are an Evidence of its Antiquity, of which according to our usual Method we shall first confider it's Church.

The CHURCH.

THis Church dedicated to St. *Nicholas*, we are well Affur'd, is very Ancient, tho after all our Pains we cannot Difcover its Founder, or the time when 'twas Built, therefore we must venture to give our Conjectures from the Architecture of it, &c as we have done in other Places Upon a careful furvey of the Structure of this Church, we find in it Three or Four diftinct kinds of Building, between every one of which by their different appearances, there must have been a confiderable Interval That which appears most Ancient is the North Wall, the lower parts of which, we suppose to have continued ever since its first Foundation This is built with Flint and Chalk Stones, and is of a great Thickness, tho' without any Care or Order, and seems of a Piece with the Buildings of the Twelfth or Thirteenth Century We have further Reason to believe it of such a standing, because there is a Cup belonging to this Church, us'd in the Communion Service call'd St *Nicholas's* Cup, of a very Antique Form, which probably was dedicated to the said Saint with the Church But that which ftrengthens this Conjecture most, is the Architecture of the Tower at the Eaft End, which feems to be Built at leaft Two or Three Hundred Years, since the Foundation of the Church, and we are affur'd is of about Three Hundred Years ftanding, the Founder dying in the Year 1425, as appears by this Inscription on a Marble Stone near the Belfry, -----
' Mr *William Bordale* principal Vicar of this Church of *Chifwick*, was Founder of the Steple
' of the fame He dyed in the Year of our Lord MCCCCXXXV both of which appears in
' the Brafs of his Tombftone in this Church This Monument of this worthy Benefactor,
' being by *William Walker* his Succeffor happily preferv'd from being loft, is now in this
' Stone commended to the lafting Memory of Pofterity, by the Right Honourable and truly
' Noble Lord, *Francis* Lord *Ruffel* Earl of *Bedford Anno Domini* MDCXXX--- The faid
Plate referr'd to in this Infcription is now in being, and the Infcription on it inferted in the
Collection following In fome other parts of this Church, the Walls feem to be Rebuilt
almoft from the Foundation, and confideribly Rais'd in feveral Places, as also Alterations
in the Windows, which feems to be done about 150 Years Ago, but that which is moft
Modern, is the South Ifle, a handfome brick Building carried a confiderable way from the
Body of the Church towards the South, Built from the Ground by the Parifhioners in the
Years, 1649, 50, and 51. (the South fide of the Church being then in a Shatter'd Condition,
and

and the Congregation much Augmented,) and coft them with some other Repairs Two Hundred Seventy Nine Pounds These are all the Alterations and Reparations we can difcover in this Church, except fome Repairs of the Chancel, by the Right Honourable Thomas Earl of Falkenberg in the Year 1694, by virtue of his Leafe from the Dean and Chapter of St Paul's

It may not be improper here to add (before we difmifs this Subject) that fome few Years after repairing of the Church, the Parifhioners likewife liberally contributed towards the rebuilding the Parfonage Houfe, which was in a very fhatter'd Condition, and in the Year 1658, the Old one was pull'd down, and a New one Erected, built of Brick very handfome and Commodious, the Parifh rate for this was Two Hundred and Sixty Pounds Alfo in the Year 1698, the Houfe being out of Repair, and wanting feveral Conveniences, it was repaired, beautified, and had fome additional Buildings added, which coft in all Fifty Six Pounds Sixteen Shillings Several of the Honourable and Eminent Inhabitants contributing very largely, particularly that Worthy Gentleman Sir Stephen Fox, who alfo at his own Charge has Built a fpacious Barn of brick near adjoyning for the ufe of the Vicar, which coft him Forty Pounds

The Infcriptions &c

In the Chancel

On the right Hand.

Sib. Vivens, & Mariæ Uxori Chariffimæ Optatæ Mortuæ (ne Quos vivus Amor & Felix concordia Conjunxit, mors ipfa divideret tumulo, hic Uxoris cineres expectant viri, (Quod vivere non licuit diu) qui Unummes Fuiffent Semper, una effe Poffint in Terra, ufque dum in Cælis Deus erit Omnia in Omnibus, Will. Walkerus hujus Ecclefiæ Paftor indignus Quod nollet, id volens pofuit, quin fibi, quodque Conjug.que fuæ Secundæ Marthæ Filiæ clariffimi Domini D Johannis Allot Equitis Aurati, & Prætoris olim Londinenfis. Deo Annuente Defignat.

And on the fame Monument follows in Englifh

Marie Walker Daughter of that Venerable Divine Mr *Robert Kay*, who honoured his Profeffion, and profited the People of *Ware* in *Hartfordfhire*, with his fruitful Preaching, and holy Life for above 60 &c. and the Wife of *William Walker* the Paftor of this Parifh was a Sampler of true Piety, Virtue and Goodnefs, endowed with much Beauty of Body, and more of Mind. She left Two Sons *Francis*, and *Theophilus*, and Four Daughters, *Mary, Faith, Anne, Elizabeth Walkers*. She liv'd beloved, and dyed defired of all, and living dayly dying, did dying come to live Eternally She finifhed the laft Year of her Mortification on Earth by Death, and entred into true Life in Heaven *Feb.* 21 *Anno Domini* 1619, *Ætatis Suæ* 41.

And underneath on the Verge of the Monument
Thy Law will I make my Will and Walk aright,
The former part of the Infcription in Englifh.

Living to himfelf, and to *Mary* his dearly beloved Wife now Dead, (leaft Death fhould divide them by the Grave, whom when alive mutual Love and reciprocal Affection made one) Here the Afhes of the Wife wait for thofe of the Husband, that as they were one in Life (which they were not permitted to be long) fo they might he together is one in the Grave, till that time, when the Almighty in the Heavens fhall be all in all) *Will Walker* the (unworthy) Minifter of this Church, willingly Built this for himfelf, and his Second Wife *Martha* Daughter of the famous Sir *John Allot* Kt formerly Lord Mayor of *London* With Gods leave he Defigns ——

On a plain Monument

Here lyeth the Body of *Anne Barker* of *Chifwick*, Widow, Daughter of *Lawrence Stoughton* of *Stoughton* in *Surrey* Efq, firft married to *Richard Mavey* of *Salinge* in the County of *Effex* Efq, by whom fhe had Six Sonnes, and Five Daughters, and having liv'd his Wife and Widow -------- and Five Years departed this Life the Fourteenth of *May*, in the Threefcore and Nineteenth Year of her Age. *Anno Domini*, 1607.

Non violenta rapit te mors fed tempore pleno,
Plena annis, meritis plenior Anna Cadis
Utque annis abfumpta cadis fic furgis in altum,
Et vivas meritis non moritura tuis
Hic igitur placide fælix Anus, offa quiefcant
Laus inter virtuos mens fuper aftra volet

In Englifh thus

Untimely Death hurries you not away,
But full of Years, of Merit full you fall ,
And as you fall, you mount and foar on high,
And Live for ever on the Wings of Fame
Here let your Bones, then Happy Woman reft
But may your Name foar up above the Stars

Under the laft, on an Ancient Monument of Alabafter

Here lyeth buried the Body of *Thomas Barker* of *Chifwick* Efq, one of his Majefties Juftices of the Peace for the County of *Middlefex*, and Bencher of the Honourable Society of the *Middle Temple London* , and Son of *William Barker* of *Sunninge* in the County of *Berks* Efq; and *Anne* his Wife, whofe Body alfo lyeth here buried He married *Mary* the Daughter of *Valentine Sanders* Efq, one of the Six Clarks of his Majefties high Court of Chancery, by whom he left Three Sons and Five Daughters He lived a faithful Member of God's Church, an Honour to his Houfe and Family, a Father to the Poor, Learned in his Profeffion, beloved of his Neighbours, and full of Days and good Works. He departed this Life, and changed his Abode here for a perpetual Manfion not made with Hands, but Eternal in the Heavens Upon the Third Day of *April*, in the Threefcore and Fifth Year of his Age *Anno Dom* 1630

On the left Hand, in the Chancel

On a plain Stone againft the Wall a confiderable diftance from the Ground, the following Infcription

Here before lyeth buried the Body of *Chidioke Wardour* Efq, who ferv'd the State in the time of Queen *Elizabeth* of famous Memory , and the moft renown'd King *James* that now is, by the fpace of Forty Two Years in the Office of Lord Treafurers Clerke, Writer of the Records of the Pells of Introitus & Exit. Who dyed the 14th Day of *September Anno Domini* 1611
And of *Mary Becker* Wiffe of the faid *Edward Wardour*, Daughter unto that Worthy Gentleman *Henry Becker*, late an Alderman of the famous City of *London*, who dyed the 19th Day of *September* 1600 Whych faid *Charles* and *Mary* had Iffue, one Sonne named *Edward*, and Three Daughters, whereof the Eldeft named *Joan*, and the Youngeft named *Ufful* died Young, but the Second named *Elizabeth*, after fhe had been married by the fpace of Tenn Years unto Sir *Stephen Lefieur* Knt now Embaffadour from the Kings Majefty unto *Mathias* II Elected Emperor of the Romans, by whom fhe had Iffue Two Sons *Edward* and *Stephen* who both dyed Infants She alfo dyed the firft Day of *April* 1606 and lyeth here buried,
As alfo the Body of *Edward Warder* Eldeft Son of *Edward* the Son of the faid *Charles* and *Mary*, **who** dyed the 11th Day of *March*, 1605

In happy Memory of all which *(viz.)* his Father, Mother, Sister and Son *Edward Warder* Esq, hath dedicated this Monument the first Day of *November* 1612, not doubting but that all their Souls do rest happily in the Kingdom of Heaven, where he doth assuredly hope he shall see them Face to Face, and also be made an Heir of the same Kingdom, through the only Merits and Mercies of our Lord and Saviour *Jesus Christ*

In the Chancel Pavement

On a brass Plate the following Inscription in the Old English Character.

Here lyeth interred the Corpes of *Mary Bateott* Daughter of *John Bateott* Esq, Pensioner unto our most gratious Queene *Elizabeth,* and Wyffe unto *Richard Barker* of *Semnige* Esq, and with her *Anne Barker* her Vth Child of whom she died in Childbed, and at her Death leaving a Sonne and a Daughter living She dyed the viith Day of *November* whose Soul assuredly resteth with the Lord, and her Bodie upon that suddain occasion buried the ixth Day - ------ *Anno Domini* MDXCIX
   Et regni Reg.næ Elizabethæ quadragessimo primo

On a black Marble Stone near adjoyning these Words.

 MARCUS ANTONIUS La Bastide
 De Crosat Obiit Quarto Martii Anno 1704.

This Gentleman was Secretary to the Marquiss Rovigny Ambassador from the King of *France* to *Oliver Cromwel.*

Part of the following Inscription is hid by the Chancel Rails.

Here lyeth Interred the Body of Mr *Tho. Elborour* late Vicar of *Chiswick* He departed this Life the Seventh Day of *April* Aged 54

In the Middle Isle on a very old brass Plate, now in the Hands of the Church Wardens, the Impressions of which is Visible upon an Old Stone, to which it belong'd, is the following Inscriptions before Mention'd

 Hic jacet Willius Bordale Principalis Vicari hujus ecclie & Fundator campan les ejusd Qui Obit xvth. die Mess Octobris, Anno Domini MCCCCXXXV, *cujus aie propicietur Deus Amen.*

In English thus

Here lyes *William Bordale* principal Vicar of this Church, and Founder of the Steeple. Who dyed 15 Day of *October* 1435 to whose Soul God be Merciful, *Amen*

This Inscription Mr *Weever* takes Notice of in his Funeral Monuments, and imperfectly Transcribes, he mentions another which next follows, tho now Defaced, and must no doubt on't omit many more then in being.

 Orate pro anima Mithildis Salwyne uxoris Richardi Salwyne Militis Thesaur.... Ed ----- qui Obiit 1437

In the South Isle

On a very beautiful Monument of Black and white Marble

Near this place lyeth interred the Body of *Richard Tayler* Esq, late Inhabitant of this Parish, in a Vault Built by him and appropriated to his own Family *Obiit 29 August 1698 Etat 73* Also *Richard* and *Anne Tyler* Children of their eldest Son RT Jr at Akis present.

A Barely

A ftately Modern Tablet of white Marble near ro Foot in length. The Architrave, &c
fupported by Two Ionick black Marble Pillars At the Top ftands an Urn from whence
hang Feftoons. This coft Fifty Pound.

M S

Near this Place lyes the Body of *James Howard* Efq, only son
of the Honourable *Thomas Howard*, Brother to the Right Honourable *James* Earl of *Suffolk*, who was interr'd the 6th Day of
July 166) About the 20th Year of his Age

In the Chancel near the Pulpit an antient Monument of Alabafter, having the Effigies of
Sir *Thomas Chaloner* and his Lady kneeling, beautified with feveral neat Antique Performances. On a plate is this Infcription

Here lieth the Body of Sir *Thomas Chaloner*, who was knighted
in the Wairs of *France*, by King *Henry* the IV *Anno* 1591 and
afterwards Governour in the Minority, and Chamberlayne to
the late Prince of famous Memory, *Henry* Prince of *Wales*, Duke
of *Cornwall* and Earl of *Chefter* And he married to his firft
Wife, *Elizabeth* Daughter to *William Fleetwood* Serjeant at Law
to Queen *Elizabeth*, and Recorder of *London*, by whom he had
Iffue *Thomas* Deceas'd, *William, Edward, Thomas, Henry*, Deceas'd
Arthur Deceas'd, *James, Elizabeth* Deceas'd, *Mary*, Wife to
Sir *Edward Fifher* Knight, *Elizabeth* and *Dorothy*, and dyed the
22d Day of *June Anno Domini* 1603, aged 35 Years And to
his Second Wife he married *Judeth* Daughter to *William Blunt*
of *London* Efq, by whom he had alfo Iffue *Henry, Charles, Fre-
dericke* and *Arthur Anne, Katherine*, and *Frances*, and fhe Deceas'd the
30th of *June Anno Domini* 1615, aged 36 Years And the
aforefaid Sir *Thomas Chaloner* dyed the 18th Day of *November*
1615, being of the Age of 51 Years

There is little Occafion for the Character of this great Man, his being appointed Preceptor to Prince *Henry*, by that Learned and judicious Prince King *James* I is a fufficient Evidence of his great Abilities and exemplary Virtues He was as univerfally Learned as he
was efteem'd, a Complete Gentleman, and an Experienc'd Soldier He was a great Natura-
lift, and very curious in his Enquiries, as appears by the Difcovery he made of the Alum
and Coperas Mines at *Gifburgh* in *Yorkfhire* [*Camden Brit* pa 753] Where the Family at
this Day (if we are not misinform'd) ftill Flourifh

Of the ADVOWSON and Mannors

THE right of Prefentation to this Living is originally in the Dean and Chapter of St *Pauls*,
and by them was lett with the great Tythes, and their Mannor to the late Earl of
Falconberg and is now in the Hands of his Lady the Countefs Dowager of that Place

This Vicarage is valued in the Queens Book bat it Seventeen Pounds Nineteen Shillings
and Two Pence, but is thought worth about one Hundred and Fifty Pounds *per Annum*, to the
Reverend Mr *James Ellaby* the prefent worthy Vicar.

This Parifh contains Two Mannors, viz one call'd the Deans Mannor, having a fine
Houfe, and Gardens at *Sutton-court*, let is before to the Lord *Falkenberg*, and is faid to be worth
above Three Hundred Pound *per Annum* The other call'd the Prebends Mannor, belonging
to the Prebends of *Wefmunfter*, is lett by them to Sir *Stephen Fox* Knight

The TOWN

THO' but fmall, is fo very pleafantly fituated out of the Road, and free from Noife, Duft
and Hurry, that it has for many Years paft, boafted of more Illuftrious and Noble
Perfons than any of his Neighbours, nor is it at prefent without a good Number of Perfons of
great Quality and Worth The *Thames* taking an Oblique Courfe from *Fulham* and *Hammerfmith*, but gently Salutes this Place, and the feveral little Iflands, or Eights fo pleafantly
fcattered in it contiderably weakens its force The greateft Number of Houfes are fituated
along by the Water fide from the Lyme Hill near *Hammerfmith* to the Church, in which
dwell feveral fmall Traders, but for the moft part Fifhermen and Watermen, who make an
confiderable part of the Inhabitants of this Town There is alfo North of the Church a
large Street with fome handfome Buildings, and pleafant Gardens belonging to them and
to the North Weft feveral noble Seats Near the Church, upon the *Tace* fide, is a very
antient Houfe, [*Sir Bp* pa 2] which *Norden* calls this one, and fays it belong'd to

》 t to a

Dr *Goodman* Dean of *Weſtminſter*, where the Schollars of that School in time of any common Plague, or Sickneſs, as alſo to take the Air, us'd to retire. Dr *Busby* with ſome of his School us'd frequently in Summer time to ſpend ſome time here, but the Building is now ſo decay'd with Age, that 'tis unfit for ſuch a uſe, and is patch'd up into ſmall Tenements for the poor labouring People of the Town. We can't gather who was Founder of this Structure, or what 'twas deſign'd for, but upon a careful Examination of it by the Dimenſions and Contrivance of it, it ſeems to have been intended for a religious Uſe. Here are alſo ſeveral other dwelling Houſes which appear very Antient, in which there are ſome Ornaments in the Wainſcot and Cieling very Curious and Elaborate, and of a conſiderable ſtanding.

The fine Seats, Villages and conſiderable Inhabitants, &c.

I. IN a Lane North-eaſt of the Church is a noble antient Seat built by Sir *Edward Warden*, after the antient Manner very regular and Strong. It has many very ſpacious Rooms in it, and large Gardens behind. In this Seat formerly dwelt *James* Duke of *Monmouth*, it afterwards was purchas'd by the Right Honourable the Earl of *Burlington* where he liv'd and Dy'd, his Son the late Earl us'd commonly to dwell there during the Summer Seaſon.

II. Next adjoyning is a very Beautiful Seat, Built by Sir *Stephen Fox* after the Modern Manner, the Model being altogether New.

This Houſe is large and extraordinary well Finiſh'd, nor does it ſtoop for fine Furniture, curious Painting, &c. to many in England. In the Compartment at the South Door is good Painting in Freſco, alſo adjoyning are ſeveral handſome, ſtately Offices, as Kitchen, Servants Lodgings, Coach-houſes and Stables, &c. which look like ſo many Gentlemens Seats. The Gardens are extraordinary fine, and the Collection very curious and coſtly. In fine, here is nothing wanting to make it a compleat, pleaſant Seat, and the Hoſpitality within, is equal to the Magnificence without, and both worthy of the Bounty of that much eſteem'd Gentleman Sir *Stephen Fox*, who generally reſides here the greateſt part of the Year. Who after having been employ'd in ſeveral Poſts of greateſt Honour and Truſt, and in all of them acquitted himſelf honourably, at length being conſiderably Advanc'd in Years, withdrew to this Place, to end his Days in Peace. 'Twas after the Model of this Houſe, the Earl of *Ranalaughs* at *Chelſea* was Built.

Near Sir *Stephens* Seat is an antient Houſe in which dwells ——

III. Alſo at *Sutton Court* at the Mannor Houſe the Counteſs Dowager of *Falconberg*. The Houſe is pleaſantly ſituated, and the Gardens are very curious.

To the Weſt of the Town beyond the Seat belonging to the Earl of *Burlington*, is a ſpatious Regular, Modern Building, call'd *Grove-houſe*, in which dwells *Scory Barke* Eſq; lately choſen Knight of the Shire for *Middleſex*, to ſerve in the enſuing Parliament. This Seat is pleaſantly ſituated near the *Thames* ſide, behind it are Gardens by ſome ſaid to be the fineſt in *England*, and before a ſmall Park, Encloſ'd with a large Brick Wall. This Gentlemans Anceſtors has for a long Tract of Time dwelt at this Place, and ſeveral of them lye buried in the Chancel at *Chiſwick*, as appears before.

Here was formerly a Seat belonging to the noble Family of the *Ruſſels*, which was lately Demoliſh'd, and upon the Spot where the Houſe ſtood, are ſeveral Tenements Built.

Here alſo formerly dwelt Sir *John Denham* Knight of the *Bath*, a moſt celebrated Engliſh Poet. Alſo the Right Honourable the Counteſs Dowager of *Denbigh*.

V. At *Turnham green* dwells alſo, Sir *John Charldron* in a very good Seat, with pleaſant Gardens.

VI. Alſo the Lady *Lott* in another very handſome Seat.

In *Chiſwick* alſo lives Mr *Richard Carey* Merchant, with ſome other worthy Gentlemen whoſe Names we can't readily remember.

There is but Two Villages in this Pariſh, viz. *Turnham-green*, upon the Road near *Hammerſmith*, where are ſeveral good Brick Houſes, and ſo conſiderable a number of Inhabitants, that it ſeems as big as *Chiſwick* it ſelf, and *Strandin* in the Green's ſtriggling place by the *Thames* ſide, ſtretching it ſelf almoſt to old *Brentford*, inhabited chiefly by Fiſhermen. At *Strandin* are there are a few poor Houſes, which indeed does not deſerve the Name of a Village, in all other this Pariſh are Scatter'd farm Houſes and pleaſant Seats, ſo that 'tis very populous, and conſiderably well Improv'd, and ſeems yet to be in a thriving Condition.

ACTON

STanding about a Mile North of *Chifwick*, upon a gentle rifing, was fo call'd according to Dr *Fuller*, from an Oak or Oaks, (as near Twenty other places in *England* are, of which this is the Chief,) from whence he conjectures, there were plenty of Oaks in this Place, the Soyl being very proper for that Wood, *viz.* a binding Clay, tho' there is none now growing here that are confiderable This Parifh is almoft Square, and Butts North upon *Willdon*, Laft and South-eaft, upon *Kenfington* and *Hammerfmith*, South upon *Chifwick* and Weft upon *Ealing* This fpot of Ground is generally Sow'd every Year with all forts of Grain, which 'tis very proper for, and produces kindly, fo that moft of the confiderable Inhabitants, except a few Gentlemen) are Farmers and Husbandmen We could not at one time fpent, find any remains of Antiquity here, nor any thing that was Worthy of our Notice, except its Church, the moft antient Structure in the Town, which according to our ufual Method we fhall firft Confider

The CHURCH

STands upon a fmall Afcent, and the Body of it, by the manner of Building, feems to be of about Four or Five Hundred Years ftanding 'Tis but fmall, the Windows and Doors but Narrow, and Walls very Low, and is Built of Flint and a fort of foft Stone, much us'd about the Thirteenth, Fourteenth, Fifteenth and Sixteenth Centuries The Tower at the Weft end is of a much later Date, and is built of Brick corner'd with Stone, very him fome, regular and lofty, and has in it a ring of Six Bells with Battlements, and a handfome Cupola at Top It feems much like fome Buildings of Card *Woolfey's*, and others, in the beginning of the Sixteenth Century, fo that we conclude, it was built about that time, tho', if an Ancient Inhabitant of above 100 Years of Age lately living might be believ'd, it muft be Older, for he Affirms, it feem'd as much Decay'd and Worn in his Childhood, as it does now Tradition has left nothing concerning the Dedication or Founding of this Church, nor could we get any light in thofe particulars, by turning over the Parifh Books, nor from the moft inquifitive fearch otherwife The Body of the Church being very much Decay'd, the Roof fhatter'd, and the Windows, &c much out of order, it was in the Year 1701, Repair'd by the Parifhioners, white wafh'd and very much beautify'd, the Parifh Rate amounting to Two Hundred and Thirty Pounds Ten Shillings, which feems to be the only general Repair it has had for many Years There has been feveral Perfons of Note Interr'd in this Church, whofe Monuments are kept in good Order, and have not met with fuch ill Ufage, as thofe venerable remains of our Anceftors frequently us'd to do, from the carelefs Hands of thofe Employ'd in the Repairs of Churches, however, the Saints of the Republican ftrain made the fame Havock here, as they generally did elfewhere, there being fcarce a brafs Plate left upon a Grave Stone, or Effigies of Value, but what is tore off

The Infcriptions and Monuments in this Church.

In the Chancel on the left Hand

Is an Alabafter Monument embellifh'd with feveral Figures, and other antique Performances Guilt, Erected to the Memory of the Right Honourable the Lady *Catherine*, Vicountefs of *Conway*, Wife to the Lord *Conway*, Chief Secretary of State to K. *James* and K. *Charles* I and Prefident of the Council, upon which is a large Infcription in Letters of Gold, giving an Account of her many Pious Gifts to charitable Ufes, fome of which follows, the Infcription being fo decay'd, that it could not be well Read

She gave

Ten Pounds to the Poor of *Acton* to be paid at her Funeral

Two Hundred Pounds to the Company of *Grooms, London*, upon Condition they fhould *Per Annum* for ever Pay, the Sum of Ten Pounds to the Poor of *Acton* at equal quarterly Payments

Three Hundred Pounds to the Dutch Church, to be kept as a Stock for their Poor, and the Annual Profits thereof are to be diftributed to 'em, at the Deacons Difcretion

Ten Pounds *Per Annum* more to the Poor of *Acton*, to be paid half yearly, *viz* Five Pounds at *Chriftmas*, and Five Pounds at *Whitfuntide* The firft Payment to Commence from the Death of a certain Neece of hers, who was to enjoy it during Life

Five Pounds to be diftributed at the time of her Funeral, to the Poor of the Parifh of *Paddington*

Five Pounds *Per Annum* for ever to the Poor of the faid Parifh

Twelve Pounds to *Ludgate*, and the Two Compters to be paid at her Death, *viz* Four Pounds to each for the Poor Prifoners

Also Ten Pounds *Per Annum* for ever, to the said Prisons to releafe Four Prisoners yearly, *viz.* Two out of *Ludgate*, and one out of each Compter

Twenty Pounds *Per Annum* for ever to *Chrifts Hofpital, London.*

Ten Pounds *Per Annum* for ever to the Poor of *St Dunftans* in the Eaft

Twenty Five Pounds *Per Annum* for ever to Five free *Grocers* Widows So that this Charitable Lady gave in all to pious Ufes to the Value of 2127 *l.*

Then follows.

The Poor who did thy Life with Prayers befriend,
And on thy Funeral Hearfe in Tears attend,
Shew their Devotion ftill, and fend on high
Their Prayers for thy bleffed Charity.
May thy Example others Teach to give,
That when they die, their Fame like Thine may Live

And underneath in the Pavement on a Marble Stone this Infcription;

Underneath this Marble Stone lyeth buried, the Body of the Lady *Catherine,* Vicountefs of *Conway,* the late Wife of the right Honourable, *Edward* Lord Vicount *Conway* Deceas'd, fhe being aged about 74 Years, whofe Monument is near hereunto Annexed.

The Lady here Interr'd was Married to the Right Honourable *Edward* Vicount *Conway,* defcended of an antient knightly Family His Anceftor Sir *Henry Conway* was a great Favorite of *Richard* II and his Grandfather and Father eminently fignaliz'd themfelves in the Service of their Country againft the *Scots* and *Spaniards* This Noble Peer was knighted by *Robert* Earl of *Effex,* at the facking of *Cadiz* in *Spain,* afterwards was made Governour of the *Brill.* In the 20 *Jac.* I he was made one of the principal Secretaries of State, and in the 22d of the fame King, Advanc'd to the Dignity of a Baron of this Realm, by the Title of Lord *Conway* of *Rayley* In the 2 *Car* I he was created Vicount *Killultaugh* of *Killultaugh* in *Ireland,* the next Year Vicount *Conway,* and afterwards made Lord Prefident of the Council, and fent Embaffadour unto *Germany.*

A plain Monument of black and white Marble near Ten Foot in length, made after the modern Manner, with Tufcan Columns, upon which in Letters of Gold is the following Infcription.

Here lyeth Interred the Body of *John Peryn* Efq, late Alderman of the City of *London,* and one of the Commiffioners of the Peace for the County of *Middlefex,* who by his laft Will and Teftament did (after the Deceafe of Mrs *Alice Peryn,* his loving Wife and fole Executrix,) give and bequeath, all his Lands in the Parifh of Eaft *Acton,* to pious and charitable Ufes for ever, *viz.* The Sum of 26 *l Per Annum* for ever, to maintain a weekly Lector, to be preached in the Parifh Church of *Bromyard* in the County of *Hereford,* wherein he was Born, upon *Monday* in every Week being Market Day in the Forenoon, the Preacher to have to s for each Sermon, and the Clarke to have 20 s *Per Annum* for his Attendance upon thofe Days

Unto the Free Grammar School of *Bromyard* aforefaid, the Sum of 20 s *Per Annum* for ever, to be paid unto the Mafter of the faid School for his Pains, and better Encouragement

Unto the Poor of the faid Town of *Bromyard* the Sum of 5 l *Per Annum* for ever

Unto the Poor Members of the Company of *Goldfmiths, London,* Twenty Pounds a Year for ever

Unto *Chrifts Hofpital* in *London* Ten Pounds a Year for ever, 5 Pounds thereof for the Poor Children, and the other Five Pounds for a Poor blew Coat Boy that fhall be bred a Scholar, and fent to one of the Univerfities, either *Oxford* or *Cambridge,* for his better Incouragement to Study

Unto the Poor of the Parifh of St *Vedafts Fofter* in *Fofter-Lane, London,* Five Pounds a Year for ever

Unto the Poor of the Parifh of Laft *Acton* in the County of *Middlefex,* abovefaid, Ten Pounds a Year for ever, to be diftributed every Quarter of a Year among them, at the Difcretion of the Church Wardens, and Overfeers of the Poor, for the time being

Unto

Unto the Poor of the Parish of St. *Sepulchers* without *Newgate* in *London*, the Sum of Five Pounds a Year for ever.

All which Gifts and Legacies, together with the Remains of his Lands in Fee *Adou* above said, he hath left to the Care and Trust of the Right Worshipful the Company of *Gold smiths*, *London*, whereof he was a Member, to see them faithfully perform'd, according to the true intent and meaning of his last Will and Testament Expressed. He also gave to the Relief of godly aged Orthodox Ministers, fit Objects of Charity, and poor Ministers Widows the Sum of one Hundred Pounds. He gave also to the present Relief of the poor Members of the Worshipful Company of Goldsmiths, the Sum of Twenty Pounds. Having thus inlarged himself to the Glory of God, and Relief of the Poor, he finish'd his own Course the 29th of *February*, 1656.

Unto whose Memory (as a Pledge of Conjugal Affection) his loving Wife as abovesaid erected this Monument.

This Worthy and Charitable Gentleman here Interr'd, gave away to Pious and Charitable Uses, as above, allowing the Annuities at Twenty Years Purchase each, the Sum of 2141 *l.*

A neat Monument made in Fashion as the last.

A Memorial of *Philippa* late Wife of *Francis------Rouse*, she died the 20th of *December* 57, having liv'd 85 Years.

> She is not here, the Body which she wore
> Of borrowed Earth to Earth she did Restore.
> But the chief self her Soul, she did commit,
> Into his Hands, who first created it
> Of *Martha's* Part the Practise she attain'd,
> Whilst Christ she in his Servants entertain'd ,
> Yet *Mary's* better Part did not neglect,
> But heavenly Doctrines did in Soul affect.
> She said when saving Truth deliver'd was,
> That it into her very Heart did pass
> The Thankful Songs of *David* she did Love,
> And *David's* Thankfulness desir'd to Prove
> She us'd to Pray, O Lord, a thankful Heart
> With Givings, and forgivings all impart
> She full of Mercy was towards the Poor,
> And stay'd not till they came unto her Door ;
> But the Relief to their own Doors did send,
> Glad to put forth, what she to Christ did Lend.
> And after Works of Mercy now she is
> Receiving, Mercy in Eternal Bliss.

This Gentlewoman here Interr'd was Wife to that *Rouse* which was one of King *Charles* I. Judges (if we mistake not) and a forward Instrument in the late Rebellion, in consideration of his services *Cromwell* made him one of his Lords, and his Wife was upon her Monument still'd Lady, which Title upon the Restoration of King *Charles* II was Expung'd, the spaces between the Names being still Visible.

Between the Two last a small Oval Alabaster Monument

M   S

Jonathæ Rogers Gen Filii Jonathæ Rogers de Chipenham agro. Wilton, Gent & Flizabetha Uxoris ejus, Filiæ Antonii Saunders de Eastlack agro. Gloucst S I P. qui Obiit the 4th February, 169 Ætat 21

Sacred to the Memory
Of *Jonathan Rogers* Gentleman, Son of *Jonathan Rogers* of *Chippen ham* in *Wiltshire* Gentleman, and of *Flax* his Wife, Daughter of *Anthony Saunders* of *Eastlack* in *Gloucestershire*, D D who died the 4th of *February* 169 Aged 21 Years.

On the right Hand of the Chancel

------ A Small Monument of Alabaster gilded and beautified with several Devices, and on a black stone in Letters of Gold this Inscription

Consecrated to the Memory of the Honour and Ornament of her Sex, the Lady *Anne Southwel* Eldest Daughter of Sir *Thomas*

Harris of *Cornworlie* in the County of *Devon* Knight, and Serjeant at Law, first married to Sir *Thomas Southwel* of *Pixworth* in the County of *Norfolk* Knight.

Afterwards follows a long Inscription not Legible

And on the right Hand of the said Monument on a Board is thus Written.

An Epitaph compos'd to the Eternal Memory of the Virtuous, and well qualified Lady, the Lady *Anne Southwel* deceased the 2d of *October* 1636

> Seeking for choicest attributes to raise
> A Pyramid to Lady *Southwells* Praise ;
> I found Invention of so low a flight,
> Her worth was still above my fancys Highth.
> At last comes Fame, and whispers in my Ear,
> If thou a worthy Monument would'st rear,
> Call her rare piece of Nature, soul of Art,
> Nurse of Religion, Learnings better part.
> Mirrour of Ladies, Virtues Golden Mine,
> The Graces Temple, darling of the Nine,
> Heavens Joy, Earths Wonder, Truths fair Patroness,
> Thou may'st give more, but she deserves no less
>
> H S

On a Board on the left Hand of her Monument is Written the following Inscription

To the never dying Memory of that Lady every way Worthy, the Lady *Anne Southwel*, who upon the Second of *October* in the Year of Grace 1636, and of her Age 63 slept sweetly in the Lord, these few Lines are dedicated by *Roger Cooke*, a true Lover and Admirer of her Virtue

> The SOUTH Wind blew upon a springing WELL,
> Whose Waters flowed, and the sweet stream did swell,
> To such a highth of goodness that they lent
> The lower plains a feeding Nourishment:
> Until at last like envious *Philistines*,
> Remorseless Death with restless Time combines
> To stop the Current, but victorious Fame
> Triumphs o're Death, and time, and strikes a Flame
> Out of her Ashes, which does burn so Bright,
> That shining gives the World perpetual Light.

And on a rough Stone on the other side the Chancel is a brass plate, with this single Line

Here lyeth the Body of the Lady *Anne Southwell*.

On a large black Stone in the Chancel having a Coat neatly done, is the following Elegant Inscription

> Hic *Jacet Elizabetha Ramsey*,
> Henrici *Ramsey Armigeri*
> Uxor *Charissima* ,
> Non *sibi nata, non sibi vixit*,
> Amicis *semper grata*,
> Utilis *Egenis*,
> Omnibus *Desideratissima*,
> Pietatis *tum Christianæ, tum Conjugalis*
> Religiosissime *Studiosa*,
> Marito *pariter ac Deo Fidelis* ,
> Dum *valuerit Prudentiæ*,
> Moritura *Patientiæ*
> Exemplar
> Utriusque *fortunæ Capax*
> Nec *tristis, nec Lascrva*,
> Sed antiquæ *Verecundiæ Cultrix*
> alacris *& Severa*
> Viro *felici invicem Miseroque*
> Hanc *mutuam dedere Cœli*,
> Atque *iterum rapuere suam*
> Nata *Decembris 21 1643*
> Obiit *Julii------26 1689*.
> In *piam Conjugis Memoriam*

MNHMOZYON hoc pofuit Maritus
Sua functus peregrinatione
Scripsam juxta positurus

In English thus

-----Here lyeth *Elizabeth Ramsey*, the Excellent Wife of *Henry Ramsey* Esq, she was not Born for her self, nor did she live to her self. To her Friends always agreeable, to the Poor useful, to ill persons lovely and desirable, strictly observant of her Duty, is a Christian, and as Wife, alike faithful to God, and her Husband. While she was well, a Pattern of Prudence, when Sick and about to Die, of Patience. Capable and fit for the extreams of Fortune, neither melancholly, nor light, but a true Lover of ancient Modesty. Chearful and yet severely Virtuous. Lent by Heaven to her Husband, who was as happy while he Enjoy'd her, as he was miserable when she was Snatch'd from him. She was Born the 21st of *December*, 1643
Died the 26th of *July*.———1689.
This to the Pious Memory of his Wife, by her loving Husband who purposes (when got through this foreign Country) to lay himself by her

Under the Communion Table on a white Marble Stone

Here lyes the Body of *Elizabeth* Daughter of Sir *Hele Hooke* Barronet, and *Esther* his Wife, she departed this Life the 19th. of *January*, 1688 and in the Second Year of her Age

On the right Hand against the Wall, near the Pulpit, a neat Monument of white Marble, Inclos'd with Palm Branches, &c about Six Foot in length, which Cost about Thirty Five Pounds, and on it these Lines

Heu quam brevis occidit Ætas mortalis
Catherina prima Tribus, nulli Secunda
Filia Tuom Henstow Ar apud nostrates satis Insignis.
Nec Non
Maria (Relicta Gualteri Mayle Ar) Ex Illustri
Familia stapleton de Wighill in Agro Ebor
Oriunda
H S E
Quæ Postquam XIIII Annos formâ Admodum Egregiâ,
Borâ Indole Multaque Modestiâ, suis & aliis Maxime grata
Transegerat ,
Quicquid Mortale habuit
Deposuit,
Aug 26. 1680
Mors intermittit vitam, non eripit,
Et en et iterum quæ non in lucem
R ponet Dies
I H S

Alas! How soon did the Flower of Life fade, *Catherine* the first of Three, inferiour to none, the Daughter of *Thomas Henstow* Esq, of considerable Note among us. As also of *Mary* (the Relict of *Walter Mayle* Esq,) descended of the Noble Family of the Stapletons of *Wighill* in *Yorkshire*

Who having liv'd to the Age of Fourteen Years, being in extraordinary Beauty, of a very promising Disposition, and extreamly Belov'd, is well by all that knew her, as her Relations, laid down till that she carried of Mortality about her *August* the 26th 1680

Death extinguishes not Life, only Hides it

On another beautiful Monument of white Marble curiously veined, near the last, almost of the same form and size, is thus Inscrib'd

To the Memory of Mrs *Elizabeth Searle*, Daughter and Heir of Mr *Robert Searle* of *London* Merchant. She Died the 23d of *October*, *Anno Domini* 1674. And of her Age the Twelfth

It'h Bloſſom of her Spring 'twas ſeen,
What Fruits of Grace there would have been,
But what her haſty Death deny'd,
Is now in Paradiſe Supply'd
Where there is neither Spring nor Fall,
But Summer's there perpetual
Here early Soul in Flower here,
Is Ripe to endleſs Glory there
And now her Virgin Soul's Chriſt's Bride,
And lives with him, who for her Dy'd
Her tender Duſt too at Chriſts call,
Talitha Cumi ' joyful ſhall
From the Sleep of Death Awake,
Of Life and Glory to partake

A large plain Monument adjoyning to the Pulpit, of Alabaſter upon which is as follows.

Chriſt is all in all
To the ſorrowful (yet moſt deſerved) Memory of his late Wor-
thy and well beloved Wife, Mrs. *Mary Skipon*, who paſſed thro'
Death to Life the 27th Day of the 11th. Month (vulgarly *Ja-
nuary*) the 54th of her Age, and after her Marriage, 34 Years.
In Chriſt ſhe overcame,
And now with Chriſt doth Reign

Then follows a large Account of her Life, and Piety, all in Engliſh Verſe and of the ſame
Strain, by her Husband, but ſo very inſipid, that the Fear of their being Nauſeous to our
Readers, inclin'd us to omit them. Then follows under neath theſe Four Lines

Times Head hath Hair before, but after none,
Therefore in Time, take Time, e're Time be gone.
Know Chriſt, Fear God, Fly Sin, prepare to Die,
Upon this Moment hangs Eternity.
In the middle Iſle is a large black Stone, under which ſhe lyes Buried.

On a large black Marble Stone before the Chancel in the ſaid Iſle.

Here lyes the Body of *Elizabeth Godolphin*, Daughter and Heir
to Sir *John Godolphin*, Maid of Honour to her ſacred Maieſty
the Queen, who departed this World in the 18th. Year of her
Age, and was buried *March* the 17th 1683.

Againſt the Will of the North Iſle is fixt a braſs Plate upon which is Engrav'd a Man
Kneeling before an Altar, and this Inſcription in a very old Character

Here under Fote before this Stone lyeth buried the Bodye of Humfrey
Cuett Eſquire, who departed the XVIIth of March, in the Yere of
on Lord God M,CCCC,LVIII.

In the Pavement before the Communion Table lyes a very ancient braſs Plate, with an
Inſcription in Engliſh Verſe ſtill legible, (with a little Trouble,) which is the only one now
remaining Weever Obſerves, [Funer. Mon pa 531] tho' 'tis not exactly Tranſcrib'd, nor ſpelt
by him

All you that this way by me ſal paſſe
Conſyder what I am, and whoo I was,
Byſide I was Fyſte, John by name
Here yn Acton Prieſte and Poſon of the ſame
Fyfty Yere and thre Govern dyd I here,
And fynyſhed my Lyfe yn the Too and Forty Yere,
After a Thouſand CCCC of our Lordes commyng,
In that me to Redeme by ſoor Payne ſufferyn
And now that I have payde the ſtypende of thys Lyfe,
Yeldyng my Fleſh to Wormes wytowt any ſtryſe,
For my Soule yntercede that Glory yt may opteyne
Wher wyth the bleſſed enmyte eterally yt may reyne
And for yow ageyne pray by whoſe Charyte I am relevy'd
To ſweet Jeſu, wythe whoſe holy Blude we be Redemy'd

By this the Reader has a Taſt of the Language and Poetry of our Country, about the latter end of King *Henry* VIII. Reigne, which may notwithſtanding be eſteem'd a polite Age, if compar'd with that which preceded it, when nothing like Art or Language was any where viſible, but all ſeem'd involv'd in univerſal Darkneſs.

Norden and *Weaver* both take notice of the Burial of the Baron of *Burford* in this Church, the former ſays, he lyes under a white Marble Stone, which the latter Affirms had the following Inſcription on it, tho' the Stone which Tradition calls his (upon which is an Impreſſion of a braſs Plate and the Effigies of an Armed Man) is purbeck, or very like it, nor are any Remains of the following Epitaph now left.

> Pray for the Soul of Sir *Thomas Cornwal* Baron of *Burford* in the County of *Salop* Knight and Banneret Which took to Wife *Anne*, the Daughter of Sir *Richard Corbet* of the ſame County, who departed this lyf the xixth. of *Auguſt* MDXXXVII on whoſe Soul, *&c.*

This Gentleman was caſually Interr'd here, dying in this Town, as he was going from *London* to his own Country he was not a Parliamentary, but Titular Baron, and held from the King to find five Men for the Army of *Wales*, and by Service of a Barony

There are ſeveral other Stones upon which formerly were Effigies and Inſcriptions on braſs Plates in this Church, but they being all taken away, or wretchedly defac'd, we can give the Reader no further Account of 'em

Of the ADVOWSON, *&c.*

This Living is in the Gift of the Biſhop of *London*, for the time being, who is Lord of the Mannour adjoyning

The Rectory of *Acton* is valued in the Queens Book at 14 *l.* *Per Annum*, but is ſaid to be now worth near 300

The Reverend Dr. *Anthony Saunders* is the preſent worthy Rector

---

Benefactors to the Poor, *&c.* of *Fulham* and *Hammerſmith*

Extracted from the Regiſter Book now in the Hands of the Church Wardens of *Fulham.*

DR *Ailmer* Biſhop of *London* gave 20 *l.* to the Poor of *Fulham*, which being detain'd by his Son and Executor Mr *Samuel Ailmer* above 20 Years, upon a hearing before Chancellor, *Egerton*, he was order'd to pay 40 *l.* for the ſame, which was employ'd in buying Coals   Will Dated 28 *April* 36 *Eliz.*

John Powel of *Fulham* gave to the Poor of *Fulham* Twenty Shillings

Dr *Edwards* Chancellor to the Biſhop of *London*, gave 20 *l.* to be diſtributed to the Poor of the Pariſh, and in the Codicil of his Will 100 *l.* to buy them Land, and 80 *l.* to be employ'd in repairing the Church, *&c.* Alſo long before his Death he gave 16 *l.* towards building a School Houſe, and Veſtry, at the South Porch of the Church, with Lodgings for the Maſter, and Pariſh Clarke, *&c.* He gave alſo a large Gilt Bowl for the Communion Service, with an Embroidered Pulpit Cloath and Two Cuſhions   W 9 *Jan* 1618

Mr *Thomas Griffin* of *Fulham* gave to the uſe of the Poor the Sum of Four Pounds W 8 *J* 1619

Dr *John King* Biſhop of *London* gave 20 *l.* to buy the Poor Bread, which was by the permiſſion of his Widow and Executrix, added to the 100 *l.* before given, with which was 6 *l.* Po *Annum* for ever purchaſed for the Poor   W 1 *May* 1620

Mr *Robert Jenkinſon* gave about the ſame Year the Sum of 20 *l.* to the uſe of the Poor 1620

William Day Rector alſo of *Roch* gave 30 *l.* towards augmenting the Stock of the Poor, and Two Pounds towards the Stock of the Church   W 29 *Jul* 1621

Dr *Duport* Vicar of this Pariſh gave to the Stock of the Poor   22 *Sep* 1621

Mr *Bryand Porter* Gent of *Fulham*, gave to the Poor the Sum of Five Pounds, to remain in the Stock of the Poor of *Fulham* ſide only   3 *Octob* 1622

Mr *Thomas Hall* erected and Beautified the Foot in the Church   1622

Mr *William Edwards* gave to the Poor the Sum of Ten Shillings Per *Annum* for ever, to be paid at *Midſummer* }   1 *l* d / 0 10 0

Mr *Thomas Aſhton* gave to the Poor of this Pariſh for ever Per *Annum* 1 *l* W 22 *May* 42 F.

Widow *Stevenſon* gave to the Poor of *Fulham* the Sum of Five Pounds, one half to *Fulham* ſide, and the other half to *Hammerſmith* ſide   1623

Sir *Tho. Baker* gave 20 *l.* to the Poor, one half to *Hammerſmith* ſide, and the other half to *Fulham*   W 1623

Mr *Thomas Plat* and his Wife gave Two Plates for the uſe of the Communion Table weighing both 12 Ounces 1 Penny Weight   1632

The *Lady Lumney* gave the Sum of Ten Pounds to the Poor, Quarterly to *Fulham* and Quarterly to *Hammerſmith*   1634

Sir *Simon Wilmer* gave 20 *l* to be lent to Two Young Men of *Fulham* at 6 *l Per Cent* upon Security, the produce of which *Per Annum* was to buy Bread for the Poor, under several restrictions too long to insert · *W* 1638

Mr *Japer*, lately Master of *Guilford* Hospital, left 40 *l* to be lent Gratis upon good Security to 8 Poor Traders, 4 of *Hammerfmith* and 4 of *Fulham*, at the Discretion of the Vicar and Church Wardens · *W* 12 *May* 1639

These Two last Charities (as we are inform'd) are lost

Mr. *Eubank* of *Hammerfmith* gave to the Poor of that side the Sum of 10 *l* 1620

Captain *John Saris* gave 30 *l* to buy Bread for Two such Poor as the Church Wardens should think fit, each to have a Loaf every Sunday after Sermon, till the said Sum was laid out · *W* 1648

Mr *Manning* gave for the Communion Table a Damask Table Cloth 1648

Several Parishioners gave towards furnishing the New Vestry over the Porch, with Tables and Chairs to the Value of near Four Pounds · 1656

Mr *Andrew Arnold* gave to the Poor of *Fulham* side the Sum of Forty Pounds 1655

Given by Order of the Committee of the Navy One Hundred Pounds to the Poor of *Fulham* side, to be paid by the Commissioner of the Customs, out of the Monys then in their Hands arifing from the Import of Coals , which Sum was not to be difpos'd off contrary to the Mind of Col *Edward Harvy*.

> Sign'd *John Davers*   *John Nelthorpe*
>   *John Anluby*   *Fra Leffils*
>   *Nath Hallows*

Given by another Order of the Committee for preferving the Customs for the use of the Poor of *Fulham*, the Sum of 40 *l* to be by *Ditto*, not to be difposd off without the Knowledg of *Ditto* House · 16 *Jan* 1652.

> Sign'd *John Stone*   *John Hadefley*
>   *Artho Rowfe*   *Edward Chidd*.

Mr *Nath Dancer* of *Fulham* gave the Sum of Three Pounds *Per Annum* for ever to the Poor of *Hammerfmith* and *Fulham*, to be given part Bread, and part Mony · Also 20 *l Per Annum* for ever, for Two Sermons on New Years Day, one in *Fulham* Church, and the other in *Hammerfmith* Chappel · *W* 6 *Sep* 1656.

Mr *William Ledgwick* Clerke gave to *Fulham* Poor the Sum of 15 *l*   *W* 2 *Mar* 1657

The Right Honourable Lord Vicount *Mordaunt* gave Seven Pounds Odd Mony to the Poor of *Fulham* side · 2d *Jun* 1661.

His Lady gave the Sum of Ten Pounds to *Ditto*.

Dr. *William Lord* Archbishop of *Canterbury* gave to the Poor of *Fulham* side the Sum of Five Pounds

Robert Hicks of *Fulham* Esq, give 5 *l* to buy Coals on *Fulham* side.

The Lady *Mordaunt* gave a Suit of fine Hangings for the Chancel of this Church, in 1 Carpet for the Communion Table · Also a Pulpit Cloth and Cufhion of Purple Silk Camlet Embroydered

Henry Ewyes Esq, gave 200 *l* to the Poor, to be employd for Purchafing Land for their Ufe as appears by a Claufe in his Will

Mr *Robert Blanchard* give 40 *l Per Annum* for ever, in confideration of his Afhes refting undisturb'd in this Church, viz 10 *s* to the Minifter, 5 *s* to the Church Wardens, 3 *s* to the Clarke, and 2 *s* to the Sexton, to take Care of his Body, the other 20 to be given to the Poor in Bread · *W* 1681

Sir *John Elwis* Erected the Rails round the Communion Table 1683

Thomas Winter Efq, give 10 *l Per Annum* for the Poor of *Fulham* side   *W* 8 *July* 1649

Henry Lord Bishop of *London* gave a piece of Plate for adminiftring the Bread at the Communion Table · 1684

Mrs *Anne Winter* given a piece of Plate for collecting Mony at *Ditto*.

George Clarke Efq, Built Five New Pews in the Weft Gallery of the faid Church, in confideration that the Afhes of his Relations there Interd lye undifturbd, and their Monuments are carefully preferved

So far the Register of the Parifh

Mr *Nurfe Brewno* of this Parifh gave a New Altar Piece, having *Mofes*, *Aaron*, and the Commandments, newly painted, alfo beautified with good Carving, and wainfcoted the Laft End of the Chancel, which coft him in all near 60 *l* 1676

Mr *Robert Lomp my* of this Parifh gave the Three Volumes of the Book of Martyrs, for the ufe of this Church, which are fecurd with Iron Chains under his Daughters Monument 1676

Sir *William Powell* of this Parifh founded feveral Almes-houfes in the Back-lane, for fix poor Women, who are now maintained there, by the Charity of the Lady *William*

IN the Town several Alms-houses founded by *Thomas Gouge* Gent. for 12 Poor Men and Women, who also gave a Pump for the use of the Town.

Sir *John Elwes* Kt before mention'd, founded Alms-houses for Six Poor Men and Women There is also several Alms-houses at *Paddingwick-green* founded, and handsomely Endow'd with Lands adjoyning by ------ for Six Poor Women.

Sir *Samuel Moreland* gave a Well, Pump, and Iron Ladle for publick Use, as appears by an Inscription in a Stone on the Wall, at the Gate of his late dwelling House by the Water side, lately Inhabited by Baron Nevil before mention'd, the Words are these. Sir SAMUEL MORTLAND's Well, the use of which he freely gives to all Persons ; hoping that none who shall come alter him will adventure to incur God's Displeasure by denying A CUP OF COLD WATER, (provided at anothers Cost and not their own,) to either Neighbour, Stranger, Passenger, or Poor Thirsty Beggar, *July* 8th 1695.

Benefactors to the Church and Poor, &c. of *Chiswick*.

The then Right Honourable Sir *Stephen Fox* Knight, one of the Lords Commissioners of the Treasury (a great Benefactor to this Church &c) Built, and gave to the Vicar in 1699 a handsome Substantial Barn of Brick adjoyning to the Vicarage House, which cost upwards of 40 *l* Under the said Barn is contriv'd a large Cellar, for which the Vicar receives Rent yearly, made use of by the said Worthy Gent for the laying in a large Quantity of Coals when Cheap, which in hard Weather, and Time of scarcity, he ever since has given to the Poor

The same Honourable and Worthy Benefactor, gave also the Glazing, Wainscotting, and Furniture of the Vestry House, (Built by Contribution of the Parishioners on the Vicars Soyl, on the West side of the Church) which cost him upwards of Ten Pounds He also gave very liberally towards repairing the Vicarage House, and allows every Month several Sums, for the support of Poor Ancient Persons of this Parish, &c.

The Lady ------ *Fox* first Wife of the said Sir *Stephen Fox* Kt. gave (as a New Years Gift,) a large Church Bible, and Common Prayer Book, both of Imperial Paper, and curiously Bound in Red Turkey Leather, and Gilt, as also, Two Common Prayer Books in a black Letter, Bound and Guilt after the same manner for the Communion Table, likewise Two Surplices

Mrs ------ *Fox* late Wife to the Honourable *Charles Fox* Esq, Son of the before mention'd Sir *Stephen Fox* Kt gave (in 1696) a Carpet for the Communion Table, of Rich Purple Velvet, and Two Stools Cover'd with the same, all Fring'd with Gold and Purple, also a Communion Table of Wainscot, decently Carv'd, all of which Cost upwards of Thirty Pounds.

Richard Taylor Esq, before mention'd (who lies interr'd in this Church,) gave a Pulpit Cloath and Cushion of Rich Purple Velvet, Fring'd with Gold and Purple, which Cost about Thirty Pounds

The Right Honourable *Thomas* Earl of *Falconberg*, in the Year 1700, gave for the use of the Poor by Will 80 *l* to be distributed according to the Discretion of his Executors(with the Advice of the Minister and Church-wardens) which was accordingly done in putting out Children Apprentices, &c

The Right Honourable Dame Vicountess *Shannon* gave 50 *l* to the use of the Poor of *Turnham-green*, when she Erected Mr *Howards* Monument before mention'd

Sir *Gilbert Tort* of *Turnham-green* gave by Will to the Poor 50 *l*. which was sometimes afterwards received and distributed accordingly

The Reverend Mr. *Thomas Elborough* late Vicar of this Church, gave for the Use of the Communion Table, Two large Silver Flagons, each containing Two Quarts

Mr *Henderough* gave a large Silver Bowl for the same Use Gilt, with the holy Lamb Ingrav'd on it

This Account we had from the Reverend Mr. *Ellesby* Vicar of *Chiswick*

Benefactors to the Church and Poor &c, of *Acton*.

The Right Honourable *Katherine*, Vicountess *Cornway*, gave by Will as appears on her Monument before mention'd, the Sum of Ten Pounds to be given the Poor at her Funeral, also Ten Pounds *Per Annum* for ever, to the said Poor, to be paid at Equal quarterly Payments, by the Company of Grocers *London*

Ten Pounds more *Per Annum* to be paid the said Poor, half yearly after the Death of a certain Niece of hers

This last Ten Pounds *Per Annum* was never receiv'd, (as we are inform'd the Estate proving deficient, upon the Death of the said Niece.

John Toyn Esq, of Last *Acton* in this Parish, gave by Will in 1656 as appears on his Monument before, to the Poor Ten Pounds *Per Annum* for ever to be paid quarterly.

These Benefactions above, are all that are Annual of Note, there have been, and are some other small ones, the particulars of which we could not learn

A SUPPLEMENT.

Since the printing of the preceding Sheets, several particulars have been Communicated to us, that ought to have been incerted in them, which it being too late to do now and being at the same time unwilling to deprive the World of them, we thought it might not be improper to add them here (with some Omissions made through mistake) by way of Supplement.

IULHAM

In the Church Tower is a very good Ring of Six Bells, (pa 26)

Under the Communion Table, in the Chancel, lye Interr'd in a small Vault made about Four Years Ago, the Bodies of the Honourable the Lady *Katherine Seymour*, Grandmother to his Grace the present Duke of *Sommerset*, and also of Sir *John Elwes* Knight of *Grove-house*, before mention'd her Nephew, who was one of the Justices of the Peace for the County of *Middlesex*, and Impropriator of the Living of *Fulham*, a Gent much esteem'd by all that knew him for his Integrity, Worth, and Honour (pa. 28)

Of its Advowson (pa 35) To this Living it seems belong a Rector and a Vicar, besides the Impropriator Brook Bridges Esq, The Right of Presentation is in the Reverend Dr *Thomas Turner* Rector, and not in *James Bridges* Esq, as is before express'd by Mistake, and the Reverend Mr *Vincent Barry*, and not Mr *William*, is Vicar.

The Seats and considerable Inhabitants. The Ancient Seat said (pa 37) to belong to Sir *Joseph Williamson*, &c is call'd *Munster-House*, and belongs to Sir *John Williamson* or ------- *Williamson* Esq, his Son

There are also several other very considerable Inhabitants in this Town, as Sir *Humphry Mackworth* Kt. in a handsome Seat by the Water Side, Sir *Edward Frwin* Kt The Honourable Sir *John Stanley* Barronet, *Bernard Turner* Esq, *Robert Limpony* Gent in a Neat Seat in Church-lane, whose Estate is so Considerable in this Parish, that he is commonly call'd Lord of *Fulham*, *Henry Marsh* Gent. *Thomas King* Gent Mr *Wilson*, and Mr. *Saunders* Brewer

Parsons-Green, this Place received its Name probably from the Parsonage House now standing on it, in which dwells Mr *Thomas Carter* Gent This House in which the Rectors of *Fulham* us'd to reside, is now very Old and much decay'd, but by the Care that has been lately taken of it, is in good Tennantable Condition. There is adjoyning to it an Old Stone Building, which seems to be of about 3 or 400 Years standing, and Design'd for Religious Use, in all probability a Chappel for the Rectors and their Domesticks, which might be many in Number, this Living being worth some Ages since, above 800 *l Per Annum*, which Building is now let in Tenements Before the said House is a large Common, which within the Memory of several Ancient Inhabitants, now Living, was us'd for a Bowling green, belonging to the said Rector, and serv'd for his own, and Domesticks Diversion, from whence tis most likely the Place was Literally Call'd *Parsons-Green*

Here also stands an Ancient Seat belonging to Mrs *Aurelia Hicks* Wife of Alderman *Hicks* Deceas'd

There are several other small Villages in this Parish besides those Mention'd (pa 37) viz

Paddingswick-Green, where is an Ancient well Built Seat, in which some time since dwelt, *Mr ym him Beard* Gent, and is now in Possession of his Family

Another handsome House belonging to ------ *Bernard* Gent. of *Doctors Commons*

Mr *Tho Greog* Attorney at Law, and Mrs *Margaret Racket* dwells here likewise in very large Ancient Houses.

Also *Brook Green*, where dwells *General Johnson* Esq, Mr *Downing* and, in a very Ancient Seat, Mr *John King*

There is also a handsome Ancient Seat in *Fulham* Field, call'd, *Normand-land house*, now belonging to ------ *Wild* Esq, and at North end is now standing an Ancient Seat, in which dwells *Thomas Landry* Esq, where for many Years that Family have Flourish'd

CHISWICK

IN the Church Yard on the Vicars Soyl is lately Built a Vestry House at the Joynt Charge of the Parishioners, the Rate amounting to upwards of 40 *l*

Near the Old Building call'd the Colledge by the Water side before mention'd, is an Ancient Seat belonging to the Master of *Westminster* School, where he sometimes retires for his Diversion

ACTON

Situated as before on a gentle rising, is about Two Miles from the *Thames*, and Six from *London*

It is Blefs'd with a very fweet Air, and has feveral pleafant Walks round it. The Profpects of it are very entertaining, the Pleafant Corn Fields, Green Meadows, and handfome Shades, being nearly Checquer'd, and the feveral Fine Seats around appearing through the Trees, the gentle Courfe of the *Thames*, and the great Number of all forts of Cattle fprinkled on its verdant Banks, render the View in Summer very Delectable   The Soyl about this Town, being very proper for producing kindly all forts of Grain, as is before hinted, the Inhabitants of it are generally inclin'd to Husbandry, and Blefs'd with good Crops of all kind, efpecially of Peafe   It cannot be expected, where few but Farmers dwell, the Houfes fhould be fo ftately and regular, as in a Town Inhabited by Merchants and Oppulent Traders, the Inclinations of the former, being rather to have their Lands well Manur'd and Stock'd, and their Barns Fill'd, than to make glittering outward appearances The buildings therefore here the Reader may expect are but Ordinary, being for the moft part of Timber and Plaifter after the Ancient Manner, and confifts of but one Street through which the Road lies, befides a few Houfes ftanding in a turning beyond the Church to the Right, and fome other Buildings in a Bye Road behind it   The Road pafling through this Town, here are feveral publick Houfes, and fome good Inns for the Accommodation of Travellers, which with fome Smiths, Wheelers, Bakers, with the Husbandmen and a few Gentlemen, make up the Inhabitants of this Town   The Air, Situation, and Profpects being fo good, it may reafonably be fuppos'd here muft be fome Seats of Note, which, with their Inhabitants, we fhall next confider

Of the Seats, &c

I A Handfome Houfe, low, but regularly Built, with fine Gardens and an extraordinary Collection of Choice Plants, at the Eaft Entrance of the Town, lately belonging to the late Marquefs of *Hallifax*, to which he us'd to retreat in Summer 'Tis Inhabited now by a Gentleman of Worth, whofe Name don't readily occur to our Memory

II. In the faid Lane behind the Church are Two handfome well Built Houfes, with good Gardens, alfo in the Church Yard is a large Brick Houfe, in which for fome Years paft, the Right Honourable the Countefs Dowager of *Lucefto*, has fpent the Summers

III In the faid Lane near adjoyning, is an Ancient Houfe belonging to the Rector of this Church, with a good Garden, in which dwells the Reverend and Learned *Arthur Saunders* D D a Gentleman of known Abilities and Worth   Near this fpot lately ftood a Handfome Pile where the Learned and Pious Sir *Mathew Hale* Kt Lord Chief Juftice of the Kings Bench, us'd to refide in Summer, whofe Memory is ftill Dear to this Town, as well as to all good Men but this Seat is now quite Demolifh'd

IV At fome Diftance to the Eaft at a fmall Village call'd *Eaft-Alton*, is a Handfome Seat with good Gardens, formerly belonging to Alderman *Peryn* before mention'd, now to —— *Lamb* Efq, who fometime fince Purchas'd it, with a good Eftate Round it   Alfo near adjoyning is a famous Mineral Spring, well known for its Medicinal Virtues in *London*   There are feveral other Perfons whofe Names we can't infert, being confin'd to the narrow Limits of this Sheet

The End of the Second Part.

ADVERTISEMENT.

IN the preceding Sheets, the Reader may have obferv'd fome Words and Sentences of which he could not make Sence, efpecially among the Latin Epitaphs. This is to acquaint him, that the Tranfcriber in this Collection, did not allow himfelf a Liberty of making Conjectures (in fuch cafes) at the fence, but thought himfelf oblig'd, as near as he cou'd, to make an exact Tranfcript; therefore hopes, the miftakes of the Carver, &c. will not be laid to his Charge. Alfo in many Ancient Monuments fome Points, Letters, and Words, were fo worn, that they were not vifible, fome of which he has left untouch'd, and in others, where he has ventur'd to guefs at them, he humbly hopes the Reader will make a candid conftruction.

ERRATA'S,

Which have happen'd by the Writers Abfence, and Overfight of the Prefs, (which with the Literal Faults, &c.) the Reader is defir'd to Correct

Page 29 line 23 from the bottom for Mr read Mrs p. 31 l 17 r. Conjugalis, p 33 l 23 from the bottom, after Kneeling add, the Monument done, Ib l 10 from the bottom r. bang for buying, p. 34 L 21, omit (the) p 36 l 5 from the bottom after Camden B add laft Edition p. 37 l 14 for Weft r laft, Ib l 35 r Lemon Rebow Efq, Ib. 47, thefe Words (which bears a Yellow Tulip) in a Parenthefis, p. 38 l 2 for Eaft r. Weft, p 40 l 17 from the bottom, after Six, add other, and for fomes fence, p 41 l 20 r Edward Wolley D D and Mary his Wife, p 42 l 2 r. Compt de Normant, Ib. l 11 before Halley, omit Mr p 46 l 12 r funning, p 7 l 6 from the bottom for thill r Kiln, p 48 l 22 r Barker, Ib. l 12 from the bottom r. Sharedin, Ib l 10 r. Loft, p 49 l 24 r aflamed, p 54 l 7 for Here r Her, p 56 l 4 omit yearly, l 9 after Poor, add People, l 12 for Maun in, r Munning, l 34 from the bottom, for 20 l r 2 l, line 32 for Ledgwick r. Sedgwick

9 781379 545057